CW00381613

TTL is an imprint of
**Take That Ltd.**
**P.O.Box 200,**
**Harrogate**
**HG1 2YR**
**ENGLAND**

email:sales@takethat.co.uk

**www.takethat.co.uk**

Copyright © 2001 Take That Ltd.
Text Copyright © 2001 Terry Carroll, Mark Webb and Mark Griffith

10 9 8 7 6 5 4 3 2 1

ISBN: 1-873668-37-6

All rights reserved around the world. This publication is copyright and may not be reproduced, in whole or in part, in any manner (except for excerpts thereof for bona fide purposes in accordance with the Copyright Act) without the prior consent in writing from the Publisher.

10 9 8 7 6 5 4 3 2 1

**Trademarks:**
Trademarked names are used throughout this book. Rather than place a trademark symbol in every occurance of a trademark name, the names are being used only in an editorial fashion for the benefit of the trademark owner, with no intention to infringe the trademark.

Printed and bound in The United Kingdom.

**Disclaimer:**
The information in this publication is distributed on an "as is" basis, without warranty. While very effort has been made to ensure that this book is free from errors or omissions, neither the author, the publisher, or their respective employees and agents, shall have any liability to any person or entity with respect to any liability, loss or damage caused or alleged to have been caused directly or indirectly by advice or instructions contained in this book or by the computer hardware or software products described herein. **Readers are urged to seek prior expert advice before making decisions, or refraining from making decisions, based on information or advice contained in this book.**

TTL books are available at special quantity discounts to use as premiums and sales promotions. For more information, please contact the Director of Special Sales at the above address or contact your local bookshop.

# Contents

## *Acknowledgements*

So much time, effort and teamwork has gone into the preparation of this book. The idea was conceived three years ago, and it might not have come into fruition, but for the vision and commitment of Take That Ltd and the co-operation with collaborators, Mark Griffiths and Mark Webb.

I first came across Mark Webb in 1991, at Leeds Teaching Hospitals. We both had a very different approach, challenging orthodox thinking, in the interests of moving towards excellence.

Since then, our paths had taken very different routes until I needed the practical, up to the minute input of someone working at the leading edge of managing risk. The two Marks are just that. Our partnership in producing this book has been easy, highly productive and fun as well! I would like to thank them both of course.

In addition, I would like to express my deepest gratitude to some special people with whom I have worked in the last year. Cheryl Hill has believed in, supported and marketed the personal development and coaching business of *eplus*, which is now growing rapidly. Iain Crozier, Robin, Brian, Daren, George and Helen are among many at Lanarkshire Acute Trust, with whom I have shared so much quality time during the months spent preparing the text.

The two Marks would like to thank Sarah for her attention to detail when preparing the training materials for the risk simulation training sessions. From these, so much good feedback material was obtained about what is really going on in organisations when managing risk.

Also, Maxine, Natalie and Rachel for so many constructive ideas that contributed enormously to the process that has become *The Risk Factor*.

Finally from me to Heather, whose 'wackiness' and talent will lead to huge and deserved success. And of course, our children, two more Marks and Laura, with whom there can never be too much time.

➤      ➤      ➤

# PART A

# Introducing
# The Risk Factor

# 1
# What this book is about - an original approach to Risk

This book will change your perceptions of, and your approach to, the management of risk. Often seen in the past as dry and dusty or terse and technical, risk has become regarded as the premise of accountants, treasurers, insurers, auditors or risk managers. You will see in this book that we refer to *managing risk*. In the past, risk management has become synonymous with risk reduction, aversion or insurance. In this book, we advocate understanding risk at every stage of management from strategy to implementation. Above all, we show you how to make risk work for you.

Maybe risk is something that you have previously delegated to a specialist manager. Some eminent academics and authors recommend the establishment of a RMC (risk management committee). Many so-called risk consultants still use insurance questionnaires under the guise of risk assessment.

The approach used in this book is not only very different. It is tried and tested. It is highly successful and above all, it enables Directors and managers alike to understand the risks in their operations and make them work for the organisation. Minimising risk saves losses. Maximising risk can be highly costly. This book advocates optimising risk to make it work for you in creating and sustaining long-term value. This is what modern enterprise is about.

People are *The Risk Factor.* Our business approach is characterised by empowerment - creating the environment in which people's natural talent will flourish. Naturally, your responsibility is to balance this with an awareness of what's going on. This relies on knowledge – about the market place, customers, the environment and the organisation. That is what has been missing in many of the disasters and catastrophes that have occurred in the past. A holistic knowledge of risk will enhance understanding, management and results.

## Leaving behind the 'cult of the amateur'

Business management has come a long way in the last 20 years or so. In 1982, Rosabeth Moss Kanter first used the word empowerment. In the early 'nanosecond nineties' Tom Peters told us we lived in the age of 'brainware' even before we had got used to the 'knowledge society'. Much of British industry still thrives on the 'cult of the amateur'. It is a sad testimony that people can still reach the level of Chief Executive with little or no management training. As such, they often represent the biggest single risk to the enterprise.

Most of Western industry has tried TQM (Total Quality Management) and process re-engineering (which led to downsizing and rightsizing). While there may have been quality improvements, the costs and savings were mainly counted in terms of people.

### Risk as a differentiator in the 21st century

In the 21st century, amateurism and 'seat of the pants' management will not be enough. The growth of economic power for women and the over 50s will demand a more intuitive, stakeholder oriented, quality and care based economy. The 'cult of youth' and fashion will enhance the power of Brand. Meanwhile, risk has also emerged as a key differentiator.

The pace of change continues to accelerate. More and more people suffer from stress. An understanding of risk at every level from strategy to implementation - from the board room to the shop floo - is fundamental. The biggest single Risk Factor has become the people themselves.

Most managers have lived through half a century of 'management science'. Some people still rely on pure 'art' - intuition. Others flit from one management tool to another, with no apparent coherence, looking for the step change in success, or even resurrection. Organisations have been profligate in their use of management consultancy. This should neither be an excuse for management to abdicate responsibility for strategy, nor especially to replace key decision-making capability.

## Risk management will be pervasive

The value of management science is to augment the leadership and direction of management and help judge the best course of action, otherwise where is entrepreneurship? Management in the 21st century will be about the management of holistic risk. The winners will see only opportunity and challenge. Drucker sums it up:

"(T)here has been little work, little organised thought, little emphasis on managing an enterprise - on the risk-making, risk-taking, decision-making job.....Risk is of the essence, and risk making and risk-taking constitute the basic function of enterprise. And risks are taken not only by the general manager, but also right through the whole organisation by everybody who contributes knowledge - that is, by every manager and professional specialist. This risk is something quite different from risk in the statistician's probability; it is the risk of the unique event, the irreversible qualitative breaking of the pattern....what is lacking in the management sciences as applied today is the emphasis throughout literature and throughout its work on 'minimising risk' or even on 'eliminating risk' as the goal and ultimate purpose of its work.

"To try to eliminate risk in business enterprise is futile. Risk is inherent in the commitment of present resources to future expectations. Indeed, economic progress can be defined as the ability to take greater risks. The attempt to eliminate risks, even the attempt to minimise them, can only make them irrational and unbearable. It can only result in that greatest risk of all: rigidity.

"The main goal of a management science must be to enable businesses to take the right risk. Indeed, it must be to enable business to take greater risks - by providing knowledge and understanding of alternative risks and alternative expectations; by identifying the resources and efforts needed for desired results; by mobilising energies for contribution; and by measuring results against expectations, thereby providing means for early correction of wrong or inadequate decisions." (*Peter Drucker - Management Tasks, Responsibilities, Practices; Harper & Row, 1974*).

## *Learning from past mistakes*

What has changed in the 25 years since Drucker's book? Certainly management has taken risks, but countless examples tell of difficulty and even disaster being the result of uninformed risk, hunch, even speculation. Management has too often shown itself to be thoroughly irresponsible, or even inept. Why else in the UK did we have to resort to a series of reports and recommendations on governance by Messrs Cadbury, Hampel, Turnbull and Woolf?

Self-regulation hasn't worked because Directors and Senior Management have too often not considered risk, not been aware of it, or worst of all, have allowed unconscionable risk to prevail without enquiry, knowledge, or sound management principles.

Consideration has not been limited to corporate failure, because many so-called natural disasters have had profound consequences for organisations. Take for example the foot and mouth outbreak in the UK. Although it had limited consequences for everyday life beyond the farming and tourist industries, its huge financial costs will continue to be counted long after the recovery of tourism and the rationalisation of farming.

Go to www.bbc.co.uk and review the section on disasters, or better still, access the NASA disasters site at www.gsfc.nasa.gov/ndrd/ disaster/links not only to review the vast array of examples, but also the number which can be attributed to human error, or even incompetence.

So, there is more than enough to take account of, without adding to risks by overlooking or ignoring them. With the help of this manual, we want you and your colleagues to grasp them and use them to create lasting, differentiated success.

### Why read this risk book?

To find a more appropriate way for you and your organisation to manage risk.

There are already several texts on managing risk. So why should you read this one? There are three main reasons. First, it is very different, written in an approachable style for the non-specialist - Director, Executive, General Manager, Local Authority Officer, etc.

Second, it is time that risk was replaced by opportunity, possibility, challenge and choice. The existing texts on risk management, though detailed, comprehensive and well written, are unlikely to find much use outside the Risk Management Committee (RMC), Finance or Treasury functions.

Third, because as a Director or Executive, you will only need this book to:

> create an adaptable Strategic Plan;
> make informed choices;
> decide on business investments and developments;
> empower your people;
> design, implement and continuously and progressively improve your processes;
> commission the supporting systems;
> evaluate and manage risks;
> measure and monitor performance; and
> sleep easy at night.

A longer list appears at the end of this section.

Many books on risk eventually get into financial risk, hedging and derivatives. These are for your internal or external treasury function to manage, in a way that you can understand. Most organisations pay far higher insurance premiums than they need, rather than get appropriate risk advice that enables them to ask the right questions and help buy only the insurance they need to transfer the necessary part of a risk - saving money and enhancing earnings.

The best textbooks on risk advocate the establishment of a risk committee and complex supporting structures. These cost money, stifle initiative and slow down decision-making. Within ten years, the complex regulatory infrastructure, which many organisations have adopted in response to the Cadbury, Turnbull and Hampel reports on governance, will be abandoned. Neither industry nor government can afford such luxuries in a world where Internet fraud or the misuse of derivatives can wipe out net worth in days. Furthermore, global markets require infinitely flexible marketing and production processes, while fashion and public perception can create or destroy hard worked for brands in months.

## So what is The Risk Factor?

It is the incremental value derived from having a flexible strategic plan, that takes account of choices, fully aware of consequences, implemented by empowered people, through continuously improving processes, supported by excellent systems. Many organisations may think they can delegate risk management. We advocate the Board and top management taking responsibility for *managing risk* – which is different.

There is no need for a RMC - the Board or Executive Committee will perform this function as part of the management processes. We have gone beyond flatter structures, to infinitely evolving organisation to match processes to quality and customer preference. The virtual corporation is a fact of life in every industry. RMCs and their associated bureaucracies can be confined to the dustbin of anachronism. We cannot afford them - not just in cost terms, but also in the stifling of enterprise and empowerment.

Information, especially financial, is time dependent in value. All accuracy is spurious when a product can be developed or a market disappear in days. There is no place for passive, reactive management. We are now wholly responsible for our own destiny. For many this will be a threat. For the best it will be a series of opportunities where brand and *The Risk Factor* will differentiate the winners.

### What is so different about this book?

● *Value*

This book will create, add and sustain value in decision-making at all levels. It will enable Directors and senior management to delegate with confidence, knowing that choice will be exercised and optimised, and be especially aware of the consequences on an ongoing basis.

This book will make money and save money. It adopts a value-added approach and is long-term stakeholder value driven. It is not short-termist in any sense. It facilitates the empowerment of enterprise while retaining corporate responsibility, confident that the balance of risk and reward will be optimised.

Above all, it is based on a unique, differentiated approach, tried and tested in all sectors of enterprise, daily creating and sustaining value, whilst enhancing knowledge and enterprise. It will become the acknowledged, definitive reference and one of the few management texts that you can refer to daily.

● *Style*

This is a groundbreaking approach to the management of risk - so much so that we agonised for hours on trying to find a suitable synonym for risk, which would make crystal clear the positive, value, enhancing approach we have taken. Unlike other texts, it is neither steeped in technical language, nor do you need a degree in rocket science to understand it.

It uses a template approach, is based around a flexible strategic process and enables you to continually challenge decisions for choice and opportunity, not cost, abdication or negation. It is based on, and a basis for, objective, value enhancing questions about the enterprise. It is practical as well as strategic and not financially dominated. It is an accessible, easy to understand guide, not an academic textbook written in technical, theoretical language.

It is based on the experience and practical understanding of people who have implemented and advised on such a practical, real-world approach to risk. It is easy to read and usable. It draws on a wealth of material widely available in the UK and the US, but different from it all.

### ● *Approach*
The adopted approach starts from the point of how individuals think and work. Everyone takes conscious and unconscious risks in their personal lives every day. Just to work in the present economy and society implies risk every day, if only that of losing one's job and livelihood - and yet, stress and downshifting notwithstanding, there is still no shortage of people wishing to take such risks.

The way the corporate mind works should not be dramatically different from the way individuals think and process. After all, the corporation is a collective consciousness, ideally driven by a collective mission, towards corporate goals, in a culture of shared values not dissimilar from those we each hold. If they are, we may be divorced from the experiences and wishes of our customers, or even experience ethical or moral challenges to our decisions.

We recognise a dramatically different and fast-changing world, in the culture, style and behaviours of managers, stakeholders, business, society, individuals and government. In their own way, each is a customer. Understanding their customer attitudes, beliefs, values, preferences and behaviours is fundamental. How else can strategy optimise the opportunities and attendant risks in a positive manner, leading to positive choice and differentiating decision-making?

Despite what was said earlier, we do not advocate irresponsibility or anarchy. While respecting corporate governance and regulation, we are mindful of the mishaps, mismanagement and self-interest that led to the development of this industry of bureaucratic intervention in the free-market processes of enterprise. We would wish that society and government were even harsher on those who are incompetent, irresponsible or even criminal in their acts. Nevertheless, we believe in a free, holistic, empowering approach - entrepreneurial and value enhancing, combined with stewardship and value protection.

● *Summary of Key Elements*

There is something for everyone, in a text that is written for a dynamic, flexible, innovative, challenging 21st century world, not the unimaginative, autocratic or bureaucratic practices so often adopted in the past. The corporate sector cannot afford the cost of such inertia in terms of lost markets, let alone lost profits. The public sector cannot afford the financial costs or the loss of relevance to an increasingly self-sufficient, self-employed, discerning citizen.

We prefer to discuss challenge, opportunity and choice, rather than risk. An unceasing search for affordable quality in every process, will be the paramount requirement in the 21st century. Every risk can be recast as a risk to such quality. Art and science will come together in a holistic approach to management, with constant evaluation and re-evaluation of strategy. Value added, in every process and consistently for the long-term, will be the watchword, but awareness of the short-term threats to value will be fundamental to the daily vigil of informed and aware management.

Our approach will help you make money, as well as save money, but will also help ensure that it is reinvested wisely, in the context of known or anticipated risks, rather than constrained by a rigid, formulaic 'return on capital' constraint.

Finally, we have researched this text widely using feedback received directly from risk simulation training courses. We have also taken account of the experiences and views of many real-life practitioners, and the wealth of somewhat technical literature. It is, and will remain, bang up to date and is therefore forward looking, far seeing and relevant for the indefinite future. If you agree (or don't agree), please contact us via the web site at www.TheRiskFactor.com, or email *solvit@TheRiskFactor.com.*

Whatever your views please let us know.

## Four fundamental foundations

There is now a growing weight of literature on Risk Management. Yet, it is still a forbidding subject for those responsible for the success of the corporation and it does not merit a section in most management textbooks. Even the best risk references eventually descend into the complexities of Financial Risk, or the mundanity of administrative management and control procedures.

Above all, this book takes account of the four fundamental foundations for success in the 21st century:

> ➤ a holistic approach to business and personal life;
> ➤ the critical importance of slavish adherence to quality and continuous improvement;
> ➤ the recognition of choice (i.e. understanding and management of opportunities with a recognition of their associated risks);
> ➤ the appreciation of the value and empowerment of the individual.

With this in mind, we spent much time trying to find an alternative to the word 'risk'. That word alone inhibits the potential value protection and enhancement, which will arise from understanding and managing *The Risk Factor*.

Our conclusions were that, while we preferred to contemplate challenges and possibilities, rather than hazards and risks, the way forward was to redefine the meaning, strategic importance and differentiating potential of the holistic management of risk in the 21st century.

What did become clear was that holism, strategy, quality and choice are fundamental to the creation of lasting value in business. This was the desired context for a very different approach to managing risk. No business ought to succeed without being able to look at its strategic choices, both holistically and individually.

Traditional planning and project management methods focus on costs and benefits. Some of the more advanced corporations use forecasting, scenario planning and risk analysis and evaluation to augment this approach. Our prescription is that life and business are about realising that every decision or event arises from choice. Once accepted, this means you can achieve greater control over every aspect, aware of the possible consequences.

Nothing is achieved in life without taking a risk. Even staying in bed all day would lead to bedsores, incapacity and starvation. We are beset with challenges, possibilities, risks and consequences in everything we do. If we ignore these, we are by definition gambling. If we become preoccupied with them, we will be paralysed by indecision. The answer lies in making informed choices. If we choose to gamble, so be it, as long as we have quantified the possible outcomes, including possible elimination from the game.

As organisations and individuals, it is time to realise that destiny is in our hands. The days of incompetent, seat of the pants, management are over. The future is for those who recognise risk, rise to the challenge, maximise quality, seek continuous improvement, understand and exercise choice, innovate, flex and adapt.

It is time to take the management of risk into the mainstream, rather than delegate it to auditors, mathematicians, administrators, regulators, 'rocket scientists' and actuaries. *The Risk Factor* is about people and the decisions they make. It is about the symbiosis of opportunity, possibility, choice, consequences, risk and reward. It is about an art, supported by science, not impenetrable mathematics and jargon. It starts with a journey through history and a personal case study.

**A Practical 'Hands On' Approach to the Management of Risk**

Managing risk has, for many people had the connotations of insurance. There is a growing army of consultants offering to manage risk. Typically, at the outset of an assignment, they will use a questionnaire. It is not unusual to find that the questionnaire is based more or less on an insurance questionnaire.

*The Risk Factor* takes a quite different and more right-brain approach. It represents a practical guide to the effective handling of not only corporate risk but also risk in other sectors.

It starts by asking the question what are the Risk Factors of your business or your organisation? It provides a practical workbook approach, especially in identifying the key Risk Factors.

Often this approach is not readily accepted, indeed the people within the organisation, (particularly at a senior level where it can appear that their decisions are being questioned) can intensely dislike it.

The benefits of this approach are:
>    better services or products;
>    less waste;
>    more profit;
>    continuous quality improvement.

The by-products can include:
>    positive not negative publicity and enhancement of your brand;
>    appropriate use of costly litigation (rather than just containment);
>    more creative use of your resources; and
>    optimal management of risk.

## *Pause for Thought:*

Do you need a specific department to manage risk? What alternative is there? You could train all managers, employees and suppliers as well as those in 'partnership' in their responsibilities towards managing risk:
>    what it means to your organisation; what you expect;
>    how it integrates with all the other business or organisational activities;
>    how funding for such issues can be incorporated within departmental budgets, etc.

Our recommendation is that you split the functions of risk and insurance. Managing risk had its origins in insurance. Now it has evolved into a holistic discipline, which can be part of the fabric of organisational management. We shall return to this later.

We have heard all the advice that 'it's about 'ownership' of risk.' By all means we believe that you need to be proactive in the anticipation and management of risk. However, we believe that the mature organisation scans for and is aware of risk instinctively in every management and business process.

It's not just about managing the financial effects of risk. It's also about key matters such as quality in every risk and process, delivery and other similar outcomes. Later we shall compare the corporate organisation with the human mind, body and brain functions. 'The Risk Factor' is about people. Several chapters will be characterised by a comparison with the human individual approach and the corporate.

## *About the Authors*

● **Terry Carroll**

Terry has 'reinvented' himself in the last four years and not least through writing what is now six books. Their content and subject matter has ranged from Finance, to Treasury, trading on the Internet, NLP and personal growth. Now there is a Director level text on managing Risk.

The almost common theme is the application of right-brain thinking to what have traditionally been treated as dry, left-brain subjects. The result is a 'holistic' view.

Terry is a qualified Accountant, Banker, Stockbroker and Treasurer and, apart from their direct relevance and value to the current text, they now have no bearing on the career direction he has followed since 1997.

After 20 years in Financial Services, up to Chief Executive, he travelled through the public sector via the UK's largest NHS Trust, to reach a career totally centred on people.

First, as MD of an HR and Recruitment consultancy and now as a coach and motivational speaker, he works totally on helping people to 'fulfil their magnificent potential'. His session 'How to be Your Best' has received massive acclaim from the thousands who have attended.

Now an accepted international author, with already one book published on NLP, his consultancy brings these skills and Emotional Intelligence understanding to individuals and organisations alike. His next book will be *Be Your Best with NLP*, together with a third edition of the business best-seller: *The Role of the Finance Director*.

Terry is married to Heather (both are keen golfers), he also plays tennis and bridge, reads and writes poetry, prose and music.

● **Mark Webb**

Mark has 28 years experience of risk identification, its analysis, handling and transfer.

He trained with a major international risk carrier with responsibilities for a wide range of high profile corporate client accounts. Mark has also worked at a senior level on major strategic and implementation activity in the insurance intermediary market.

He is senior risk practitioner in a unique Risk Advisory Practice created in 1994 and a recognised expert in the public sector, for the development and implementation of strategies to handle internally retained risk whilst containing external transfer of risk.

Using his skills as a Risk Practitioner, corporate and public sector organisations have successfully 'unbundled" services delivered by the traditional market place. This enables customer clients to deal direct with risk carriers when necessary and with other specialist service providers to obtain further reductions in their costs.

It also enables the promotion of key services that deliver continual optimisation of client productivity through the progressive systematisation of handling their risks.

Mark is married to Maxine and is an avid golfer, bellringer and tennis player.

● **Mark Griffiths**

With 19 years experience of risk identification, analysis and the risk transfer market, Mark was initially recruited by a major risk transfer company. He has worked for two prominent international insurance intermediaries, developing and implementing risk transfer and handling strategies for corporate and public sector clients.

His work overseas has added an extra dimension to his understanding of risks, particularly those associated with Banking, Aerospace and Hospitals. He joined Mark Webb in 1995 as an *'in-house risk practitioner"* for a wide-ranging customer client portfolio, delivering innovative and credible alternative risk handling solutions.

A key result has been the reduction of risk transfer charges through the introduction where appropriate of direct dealing with a diverse range of suppliers. His training skills have been sought by an impressive range of customer clients to deliver their risk simulation training requirements.

Married with two children, Mark is keen on golf, gardening, travel and family life.

## *Key Questions*

There are a number of key questions, which can be asked, of the organisation in general or most practices or processes in the ordinary course of business:

➤    What is risk ?
➤    Whose responsibility is the matter in hand?
➤    How can risk be handled efficiently?
➤    What are we doing here?
➤    Why manage risk?

### Why you should read this book?

By utilising this material you will:

➤    Have a number of key 'templates' to provide a snap shot of where the organisation is on the way towards managing risk efficiently, (whatever level of the organisation you operate in);

➤ Understand what key actions need to be taken to continually move your organisation along the route of continuous and progressive improvement;

➤ Recognise the importance of links, alliances and partnerships between the management of risk and a wide range of existing processes, skills and techniques;

➤ Appreciate the importance of the many distinct yet inter-related roles, which usually exist within an organisation.

Your organisation will:

➤ Appreciate the need to 'manage risk';

➤ Understand and appreciate its significance;

➤ Have a strategy for the management of risk;

➤ Be able to create the first stage of an appropriate risk action plan;

➤ Recognise the Risk Factors facing the business;

➤ Be able to answer the question "where are we now"?

➤ Begin to recognise management of risk as an integrated role within the organisation.

### Who should read this book?

This book is of relevance to many if not most of these key roles in an organisation:

➤ Chairman;

➤ Executive Directors (all Disciplines);

➤ Non-Executive Directors;

➤ Representatives of public bodies;

➤ Managers of all disciplines;

➤ Those currently tasked with responsibility for managing risk;

➤ Those who want to be involved with the management of risk;

➤ Those who don't really want to be involved with managing risk;

➤ Those working in the corporate sector;

➤ Those working in the public sector;

➤ Those seeking a challenging career; etc…

# 2

# What is Risk?

"Risk is a threat that a company will not achieve its corporate objectives." (*The Management of Corporate Risk-a framework for directors, Harris-Jones with Bergin, ACT 1998*).

A typical dictionary definition would be 'risk is the possibility of suffering harm or loss'. Such a definition characteristically has implicit negative connotations. You will find that the present book focuses on the positive and sometimes opportunistic management of risk to anticipate, manage for and, where appropriate, capitalise on the risks inherent in any organisation.

Why is risk management so important? Traditionally, the answer would have been related to the hazards implicit in any corporate organisation and the desirability of insuring against their possible consequences. Highly visible events such as the Exxon Valdiz, Union Carbide and Barings cases as well as the Pensions and Endowment mis-selling episodes in the UK and many others, have led to a public scrutiny of the management of risks and increasing levels of new legislation. In many instances, the need for legislation has been due to previous failure to recognise or manage risks to the satisfaction of the public and shareholders.

Many professional disciplines have become progressively more objective. With the growing complexity and expense of insurance, in a climate of narrowing margins and greater cost consciousness, premiums have been reviewed and the practise of risk management has grown.

In many senses this is in keeping with prevailing stakeholder attitudes, especially shareholder objectives. Such shareholders interests are theoretically in creating long-term sustainable value. In practise, western markets have become increasingly short-termist. If this is to be believed, shareholders want their cake and to eat it. Implicitly, they require both short-term and long-term gain. The evidence is in market reaction to profit warnings, where 25 per cent or greater falls are not untypical.

What is needed is something more akin to the Japanese way: acknowledgement of the need to invest in the shorter term in order to create sustainable value. Translating this into the context of risk means the starting point is the consideration of strategy. Insurance premiums may protect against the impact of unplanned events on the profits or value creation of the enterprise. Typically, this might well involve 'events outside our control'. What we're talking about here is the human factor and the ability to plan for and manage the other key factors which, having taken account of risk, will generate the sustainable value.

Unfortunately, one of the difficulties is overcoming out dated management attitudes and ignorance. Even entrepreneurial drive does not always want to pause and contemplate risk. It may be easy, though sometimes chastening, to manage with the benefit of hindsight. It may seem easier still, to simply insure all apparently foreseeable risks. Not only is this approach potentially expensive, but in taking the thinking out of risk management it may overlook significant opportunities as well as potential hazards.

Even new issue prospectuses and company annual reports routinely consider the Risk Factors these days. We are talking here about the critical importance of 'The Risk Factor', which in our experience is based fundamentally around people. Working as a personal coach, Terry has come to the conclusion that every corporate organisational failure and every identifiable consequence or risk is in some sense based around people. Consequently, much of the coaching work is based around facilitating the understanding and resolution of the individual limitations.

Where such risks occur outside the organisation there are two possible courses of action: review the contract and/or seek appropriate recompense. Inside the organisation, every shortcoming or failure is an opportunity to learn and grow in the cycle of continuous improvement. This is true for both individuals and the organisation.

A new approach to managing risk, i.e. through awareness and understanding of the Risk Factors is becoming widespread and urgently overdue. Management by abdication is not acceptable. It is time for clearly defined and readily accepted ownership and accountability. Risk is inherent in every process or system. Understand, anticipate and manage such risks and your organisation can achieve the competitive edge that we all seek.

### The Nature of Risk

Risk is inherent in every aspect of our lives, and that includes government, organisations and corporations. Whatever their mission, vision, goals, objectives, values or standards, the risk - and its management - are inherent in the achievement or otherwise of all of them.

The domino effect – one small event knocks on to another, leading to another etc. is prominent in any consideration of risk. Often one apparently inconsequential, insignificant risk occurs causing another event, which leads to the catastrophe.

Witness the loss of NSSA's space shuttle in the 1980s, when one of the seals between the booster rocket and the fuel cell failed causing the fatal explosion. These cells had never been tested in the upright position, i.e. the position that they would be in at launch. They had only been 'bench tested" on a horizontal platform.

The problem is, no system is without risk. There was actually a myriad of risks built into the Challenger shuttle, but we can't afford perfection. While the engineers were concerned whether the seals would work at the likely temperatures, management had to make thousands of calls on other implicit or explicit risks, otherwise the shuttle would have remained on the ground. (Interestingly, the engineers rather than management paid the ultimate price).

There are over a million parts on a Boeing 747. Some are likely to fail eventually. We rely on people at every stage. People make the machine, maintain it, inspect it, fly it and manage it. There is a probability of failure to everything. Planes fly millions of miles. Buses drive millions of miles.

As we worked on this book, we heard of the shattering events in France, where an Air France Concorde crashed. There may always be a degree of speculation as to the cause, including the possibility that an error in servicing another aircraft led to a part falling off, causing a tyre to blow out on Concorde.

This extraordinary aircraft received more testing than any other aircraft in history when it was built. It has been in service for 30 years. The Russian equivalent had to be abandoned after a spectacular crash. The specific plane that crashed had undergone a yearlong overhaul in 1999.

For obvious reasons, aircraft engineering, maintenance and inspection are as rigorous as any procedures in the world. Aviation engineers, airline companies and Concorde pilots have as clear an understanding of the Risk Factors in their industry as anyone.

Leaving aside such as the Lockerbie disaster, which was the result of a terrorist bomb, there is invariably a chain of events, which ultimately destroys an aircraft. Yet again we have the 'domino effect'. Concorde was designed to fly on three engines. For whatever reason, both the starboard engines caught fire on takeoff.

When such an event occurs, it could in theory be due to a number of possible factors: physical or mechanical stress, or flaws suddenly occurring; a bird flying into the intake; a piston blade breaking; or whatever. Sometimes in similar events elsewhere in business or personal life, it is down to simple human error at some stage of the process.

Irrespective of the initial cause, this may not be the ultimate factor that brings the plane down. Concorde pilots have flown simulators where two engines fail. When you look at the wonderful record of aviation safety, you realise that where a crash has occurred, it is often on or around the time of take-off or landing.

When a pilot is taking off, or landing, there is a critical point beyond which the event cannot be aborted. If anything adverse were to happen in those few seconds, the consequences could be catastrophic. Computers can now fly planes, but often when things go wrong, they happen suddenly and they require human intervention. No matter how skilled the person is, there may be no second chances once a decision has been made.

The Risk Factors in this case went way beyond a mechanical failure or 'act of God'. Air France will have practised and simulated every possible scenario, mainly on the ground of course. When the real event occurs, as with the NSSA disaster, it may not replicate exactly the circumstances or scenarios that had been planned or prepared.

In addition, there is the risk to brand. Air France and BA that fly Concorde are highly visible airlines. Even with 'no blame' some negative publicity attaches when their 'flagship' crashes. Concorde itself may be the most visible aircraft we shall ever see. It was instantly recognised all over the world. The risk not only attached to its image, but also to whatever dreams or aspirations ordinary people have invested in the 'beautiful bird' they have seen in the sky.

The Piper Alpha disaster was entirely human error, blamed on bad communication, bad management and bad safety procedures. A valve in a pump was being routinely maintained and the work could not be completed. It was left for the night. During the night, the backup pump failed and a decision was made to revert to the other pump, where it was overlooked that the valve was missing.

An explosive cloud of gas was released and a lack of blast walls allowed rapid ignition. Oil also continued to pump in from neighbouring rigs for an hour. 167 people were killed. The danger had been highlighted 12 months earlier in a safety report but no changes had been made. This was the worst accident in offshore history.

(Note: This and many other disasters are listed in the archives of www.bbc.co.uk. Many, if not all are ultimately down to human error.)

In summary, there may be a complex domino effect of Risk Factors when disaster or catastrophe occurs, and there can sometimes be unexpected and unplanned consequences.

We have since also had the Hatfield and other rail crashes. The section of track that failed was among the busiest in the UK. One presumes it was subject to regular inspection, being on a bend on a high-speed section. Nevertheless, we understand that the rail had many small cracks in it.

We talk about 'things' failing, but there are always humans involved somewhere: humans manufacture the rail, lay the track, inspect the track and repair it. Humans drive the trains and when things go wrong, humans review the lessons to be learned. In a very meaningful way, people are ultimately the common, consistent and changeable Risk Factor.

To take a more typical example: many company directors may still tell you that they don't speculate or take financial or balance sheet risk. How many really understand that by adopting that very stance they are by definition taking the risks that they eschew. Risk is inherent in every action or non-decision the organisation takes. Financial risk is inherent in every financial decision or non-decision. To take a passive stance against interest rate risk may be just as risky as taking an active, speculative stance. We live in volatile times with volatile markets.

Risk is inherent in the fundamentals of business: strategy, its implementation and consequences. Some risks may be life threatening to the corporation, whether strategic or operational. We have cited elsewhere the example of Shell and the scenario planning that allowed them to ride out the first global oil crisis. Some organisations might have considered such a possibility as fanciful. Others might have deemed it to be outside their control.

For corporations, we are ultimately talking about investors' risk. The shareholder may have no safety net if the corporation fails (unless of course they have put in place their own individual hedge). That is the nature of equity investment. Market and specific risk are inherent. While recognising that the market risk, while it can be hedged, is beyond their control, there is a reasonable expectation that company directors and management will be aware of, and manage for, corporate risk.

Competitive risk has grown dramatically with the advent of global markets. While the range of challenges may now be seen to be beyond the wit of many managers, those who understand the principles and practice of the modern management of risk have a potential competitive edge. It starts with being able to plan for and manage the Risk Factors.

Every organisation faces practical and physical risks. These are a fact of life for us as individuals let alone as corporations. Disaster can strike at any time. Where it is truly outside our control (e.g. acts of God) we may ignore it. Otherwise, you can insure for it. Contingency and failure may be different. Contingency implies the possibility of anticipating and planning for such eventualities. Failure may be a consequence of not understanding and managing the Risk Factors.

Materiality is a significant consideration. In truth, there is little point in investing substantial resource in managing risks that are either extremely unlikely or potentially immaterial in their impact on the organisation. This is a judgement that the management has to make and we are advocating that this should be based on objective review rather than passive assumption.

Project management is becoming increasingly prevalent in corporations and organisations that are frequently having to reinvent themselves to 'stay in the game'. Operational management increasingly resembles project management. Far thinking organisations are taking managers out of the line, training them and giving them practical experience in project management and reinserting them as a future resource to draw on.

Redesign and reconstruction of the enterprise requires not only project management skills but also project risk management skills (see also business developments and investments, later). And of course, risk and the need for its appraisal are inherent in capital decisions.

### So Why is Risk Increasing in Importance?

The scale of risk is growing. Take just one aspect of modern society, litigation. For some time in the US and increasingly in western Europe, the practise is growing of resolving conflict and loss through the courts. Accidental injury, whether at work in the home or on the street is increasingly leading to claims for personal compensation. Litigation is also increasing in the field of medicine. The consequence in the National Health Service has been a widespread introduction of clinical governance. It may also in the longer-term lead to a decline in the attraction of medicine as a profession. This in itself is a risk that society will have to consider and resolve.

We have found it convenient for our purposes to identify and classify types of risk (see below). We have also introduced the concept of a Risk Factor template for understanding, managing, evaluating, ignoring, controlling and insuring risk and making informed choices as part of the daily management processes. The benefits of this approach are not just in the better understanding and management of risk, but also in greater awareness of the opportunities for success and improvement in the organisation as a whole.

The approach that we advocate in this book encourages everybody to think about and ask questions in relation to every aspect of the management and business processes. In practise, our experience has been that this results not only in a better understanding of risk but also unforeseen gains and opportunities for the corporation as a whole.

Let me use a well-known case as an illustration: Barings Bank. This case sent shock waves through the world financial markets and resulted in the collapse of one of the oldest institutions in the City of London. What might the management of Barings have done differently and what did the rest of us learn as a result? Of course, such cases can result in turmoil and loss in practice. Looked at objectively, however, they also offer many opportunities to better understand and manage corporations and organisations. Just think for a moment about changes in the market's organisations, which would not have happened without the Barings case.

Just two of the many lessons from Barings include the importance of accountability and separation of function. To what degree are the key individuals in your own organisation truly accountable? Despite all that has happened since Cadbury and Hampel, how many directors even yet understand what they are accountable, as well as responsible, for? And especially where the responsibility for managing significant sums of money exists, how many organisations have ensured that the necessary separation of function minimises the risk of loss or fraud?

These are lessons for us all and one of the aspects of this book, which characterises it throughout, is the implicit use of metaphor. While the specific examples, techniques or contexts we discuss may not at first sight appear directly relevant, every aspect is transportable to most organisations.

Companies, and indeed many other organisations, are becoming more aware of their exposures. Sometimes these exposures may not be direct. There is the case of the Scottish cashmere industry, which got caught up in the 'Banana War" between USA and Europe. Overnight, the US government imposed an arbitrary retaliatory tax, bringing the cashmere industry to its knees. The question is, would an effective programme for managing risk prepare the business for this risk? Possibly not, but a process of analysing the external risks to which the industry was exposed might well have considered the matter of tariffs.

### Categorising the Risk Factors

The Risk Factors facing business arise from many numerous and varied issues which can be grouped into the following eight key headings for ease of identification, understanding and handling:

- ➤ Technological
- ➤ Human
- ➤ Environmental
- ➤ Authoritarian
- ➤ Political
- ➤ Organisational
- ➤ Legal
- ➤ Economic

We also need to consider the difference between internal and external, global and local Risk Factors.

Each of the above categories may be further sub-divided. Below is just one set of examples. You should be able to add others that are relevant to your organisation or industry, knowledge and background.

1) The Technological Factors
   a) Developments in Computer Software
   b) Communication Techniques
   c) Buyers' increasing technical knowledge

2) The Human Factors
   a) Knowledge
   b) Responsibility
   c) Accountability

3) The Environmental Factors
   a) Ever increasing need to protect the environment
   b) Buyers' knowledge of current environmental issues
   c) Investors awareness

4) The Authoritarian Factors
   a) Central European Government Dictate
   b) Health & Safety Legislation
   c) Influence of Media Campaigns

5) The Political Factors
   a) EU - Membership and the Euro
   b) Differences between the UK political parties
   c) Differences between politics in different countries

6) The Organisational Factors
   a) Continual changes to organisational structure
   b) Reflecting evolving working practices
   c) Responding quickly to change

7) The Legal Factors
   a) Compliance with the latest laws
   b) Demonstration of compliance
   c) Balancing differing demands whilst satisfying all requirements

8) The Economic Factors
   a) Changes in standards of service reflecting buying power
   b) Fashion, fads, trends
   c) Links with sport, media and leisure

## A Typical List of Business or Organisational Risks

Ignorance and abdication can be risky and expensive in any of the following examples. They are based on the authors' practical experience working with a variety of organisations in both the private and public sectors. We have left space at the end for you to add others that you may see as relevant:

1. Absenteeism
2. Business Continuity Planning
3. Bullying
4. Business Decisions
5. Business Risks
6. Competition
7. Contingency Planning
8. Credit
9. Crisis Planning
10. Cultural v Operational
11. Currency Speculation
12. Currency Fluctuations
13. Customer Loyalty Links
14. Customer Service Issues
15. Disaster Recovery Planning
16. Engineering Risks
17. Environmental

18. Ethical
19. Financial Risk
20. Governmental Action
21. Hazard Assessment
22. Human Error
23. Health & Safety
24. Health Surveillance
25. Ignorance
26. Industrial Accidents
27. Interest Rate
28. Legal & Compliance
29. Lost Workdays
30. Occupational Hygiene
31. Occupational Disease
32. Operational Risk
33. Poor Publicity
34. Poor Record Keeping
35. Reputation & Brand
36. Regulatory Issues
37. Sickness and Absence
38. Social Concerns
39. Stress
40. Treasury Products
41. The Human Factors:
    Motivation
    Culture, and
    Organisational
42. Weather Patterns
43. ...........................
44. ...........................
45. ...........................
46. ...........................
47. ...........................
48. ...........................
49. ...........................
50...........................

Here again it is essential to your understanding that you actively participate in the process of reviewing this list to create your own personal list reflecting your organisations needs.

Our list is just a small snap-shot of one view of risk. It is included to provide the reader with a reference point. Any or all of them could occur in most organisations at any time. Many organisations have been slow to decide who 'owns" or takes responsibility for managing risk.

The question of encouraging a culture where people are willing to take responsibility and therefore managing it (risk), requires an integrated strategy, supported by a wide-ranging action plan. It needs to encompass these and other issues through integration with the management and business processes throughout the organisation.

### Four Simple Steps

It has been said that the issue of ownership is linked with incident levels. We would broaden this to propose that the management of risk is fundamentally about ownership and accountability for the management and business processes and their possible opportunities and consequences.

The risk management process can be characterised by four simple components:

➤ Evaluate

➤ Control

➤ Transfer

➤ Damage limitation (manage or minimise)

Simply defined, risk = hazard x exposure, or to put it another way, it equals possible impact multiplied by the probability of occurrence.

Managing risk is a continuous process as opposed to something that happens just once. Starting from strategy and considered throughout the organisational processes, it has potential occurrence and impacts every step of the way. The trick is in being able to see it in a positive and opportunistic way rather than a negative light.

It is true that managing risk is time consuming, but so is success or enterprise. It is important to see managing risk as a central business need woven throughout the fabric of the organisation.

**Footnote**

In the US and other countries there will be equivalents of the UK Local Authorities and NHS (National Health Service) Trusts, in public authorities and similar bodies. We work with and collectively have as much experience in such organisations as in the corporate sector. We have client organisations in both. Most of this book is applicable to all such organisations, so just a word or two may be appropriate here.

Local Authorities
Managers of risk have a low profile in many Local Authorities (LA). Breaking into the aspects of business risk can sometimes be difficult. However, LAs and other similar public sector agencies are converging and working more closely together. Governance is an issue for all organisations. It is much more satisfactory to be self-determining in this respect than to have such standards imposed from outside. Many LAs have learned from and set comparable standards to corporate sector organisations. In doing so they may often have achieved regulatory benchmarks ahead of the game.

NHS Trusts
The situation is similar in NHS Trusts. The Director of Strategy and Finance at Leeds Teaching Hospitals Trust, in 1992, was responsible for introducing strategic business planning and corporate governance long before Cadbury came along. The result was that the Trust received more favourable regulatory treatment and was better able to manage its own destiny.

➤        ➤        ➤

# 3

# The History of Risk

Whether they realised it or not, people have been taking and managing risks for all time. Records of gambling are found in ancient Egyptian hieroglyphics dating back to 3500 BC. The earliest people would take account of the weather, the stars and even the Gods, before making major decisions about battles, harvests, travel, love, etc. The word hazard comes from an ancient Arabic word - *al-zahr.* Neither gambling nor risk became prominent in society before the 17th century, however.

In 1630, 'Tulipomania' was the first financial catastrophe of modern times. Using forerunners of options, businessmen lost fortunes speculating in tulip bulbs. In the 15th century, a monk named Paccioli had invented double-entry bookkeeping, the forerunner of modern financial management, without which the management of risk could not be accounted for in business. He also posed a mathematical problem, which was only solved in 1654, by Pascal and Fermat. Their solution and debate was the origin of probability theory, which is at the heart of risk.

Despite this 300 year start, risk management had not progressed much beyond insurance and Modigliani and Miller, until relatively recently.

## A Practical Case Study

As students at Bradford Management Centre in 1970, we studied the basis of capital investment decisions. The prevalent theory was that of

Modigliani and Miller's model for valuation of the firm. It was argued that a Finance Director would take account of this in determining the capital structure.

We can now see that volatility, fund managers and resilience of earnings are more relevant. In an EVA (copyright Stern Stuart) based world, companies will simply borrow as much as they can, and repay capital out of unusable cash. Models may determine computer driven trades but not financing in a world of rapid change and profit warnings. The management of risk has little time for theory.

In 1982, the Halifax Building Society (now a UK commercial bank) set up a Treasury function. During the three years that followed, they persuaded their regulators to incorporate the use of derivatives in the 1986 Building Societies Act and commenced operations in financial risk management.

By 1986, the Finance Director of National & Provincial Building Society (now Abbey National Bank) had realised that Treasury was just a subset of risk management. (With a major financial institution, virtually all the assets and liabilities are financial). An understanding of Asset/Liability Management was developed and an originated process for 'Total Balance Sheet Management'. It was only a short step for the Board to be persuaded that they should have a strategic risk management function, analysing, understanding, evaluating and advising the organisation on the totality of its business and financial risks (i.e. a holistic view).

There was virtually no parallel for this. The nearest were the commercial risk functions of the Clearing Banks. There was no textbook on Risk Management, to stimulate thinking before designing the management processes and procedures, except for a Risk Manual. This turned out to be a practical insurance manual

Even now, the literature on managing risk is slim compared to that on finance and almost without exception, it becomes preoccupied with management of financial risk and the use of derivatives, or the detailed analysis of operational risks. This is not what Directors and senior managers either want or need.

Starting from a 'blank sheet of paper' one of the first functions in the UK for managing risk was established. This included a detailed Risk Manual, developed in partnership with every department of the organisation. The Board approved the consolidation of all aspects of financial and business risk, reporting to the Audit Committee, through the Financial Director. Over the years, this added immeasurably to the awareness of strategic, business and financial risks, with measurable benefit to the business's bottom line.

The entire organisation became 'risk aware'. When the management and business processes were re-engineered, risk was embedded within the core processes and leading edge credit and commercial risk procedures were established.

The Executive started with the strategic risk considerations, used computer simulation as a basis to evaluate and hedge net balance sheet risk and got on with running the business. Every business development or investment decision factored in risks as well as benefits, consequences and costs and the day-to-day management processes were empowered with the responsibility to include risk among the other considerations. Audit and the management of risk were converged and both operated in the nature of internal consultants, augmenting rather than inhibiting the speed and quality of decision-making.

The Board delegated responsibility for the holistic management of risk to ALCO (Asset/Liability Committee) for quantitative decisions and the Audit Committee for qualitative post-implementation review. The Executive Committee met twice a week to hear and understand business decisions, which had usually already been made. Their role was to lead the evolution of strategy and ensure continuous improvement in quality processes.

In 1991, a new Finance Director was appointed to Leeds Teaching Hospitals (now the largest NHS Trust in the UK, a complex public sector organisation with over 20,000 employees and a budget of over £300m). Within a year, a function for managing risk had been established, drawing on previous experience at a major financial services organisation. Working in partnership with the Director of a

UK Division of a major international brokerage, they saved over £250,000 in annual insurance premiums.

That partnership has now been re-established for the purpose of producing this key publication. Between us, we have over 40 years experience of strategic business management, assessing, understanding, evaluating, managing, insuring and broking risks in every sector of the economy, from SMEs to major corporate and public organisations.

### Simplicity, Opportunity and The Risk Factor

There are still relatively few companies or organisations that build risk analysis, assessment, evaluation and management considerations into daily management processes as opposed to simply insuring it. The latter, 'blind' approach, inevitably leads both to unnecessary or inflated premiums being paid. Worse still, some risks are neither being insured nor even understood before they arise and lead to serious business or financial consequences. Despite exhortations by others, you do not need a complex 'shadow' structure of RMC and supporting committees across the corporation, when considering the Risk Factor should be an inherent part of management choice and implementation.

Yet, there is a growing number of organisations, which recognise both the strategic and practical importance of 'The Risk Factor'. The old connection between risk and reward is of course true. Without taking any risk, you may eliminate or inhibit potential reward. Insurance of risk is often an abdication of responsibility and a waste of money. The key is awareness, understanding and making risk work for you.

Starting with the strategy, evaluation of risks on an ongoing basis increases the business potential, while anticipating the possible problems that can blow you off course. In the 1970s, 'scenario planning' gave Shell a competitive edge when the oil crisis happened. Far-fetched though it had seemed at the time, they had anticipated the effect of OPEC 'flexing its muscles' and had already determined the course of action.

In a practical day to day manner, leading organisations may have a function for managing risk, working across the whole business, with a holistic perspective on risks, but it should be strategic by nature, integrated into daily processes, giving advice, guidance and support rather than controlling and inhibiting choice, without an expensive existence of its own.

If it is becoming harder to justify the cost of traditional financial processes, risk control doesn't stand a chance. Facilitation is the key in a fast moving world. This approach is not designed to see what risks may trip up achievement of the agreed strategy. It mainly facilitates a better understanding of, and improvement in, the management and business processes through which the strategy is implemented.

To take just one example. Every organisation faces financial risks to their balance sheet, profitability and viability, every day. Derivatives have become an accepted factor in the management of financial risk. More and more companies are using the derivatives markets to manage or insulate these risks. Some have gone further and are speculating in the use of these instruments, increasing the overall level of risk, in the pursuit of highly leveraged rewards.

In the insurance market, derivatives are being developed and used to hedge or even 'underwrite' certain types of risk. There are textbooks devoted to this Risk Factor alone. Yet, many companies are ignorant of, or fear the use of derivatives. They are a commercial fact of life.

In the 21st century, the key differentiators between average and excellent performance will be:

> quality and customer service;

> understanding and managing risks;

> empowerment of the individual to make informed choices, aware of the possible consequences, confident of the probability of adding increasing business value.

You may become superb in every aspect of your business, but failure to understand and capitalise on 'The Risk Factor' could at least leave you financially inefficient. At best it could overlook an accessible competitive edge. At most, it could lead to net worth being destroyed by unplanned, unanticipated or, worse still, uncontrolled risks. Barings was just the tip of the iceberg! If you integrate risk consideration into daily processes, you do not need an additional layer of management to 'police' risk across the organisation.

There are already textbooks on Risk Management in the marketplace. For many, they may seem dry and impenetrable. This book is written for Directors, but will be equally valuable to senior managers. It gives a holistic perspective on risk, starting with strategy, citing the areas that Directors will wish to be aware of as part of their 'governance' function and proposing a 'template' approach to protecting and enhancing long-term value. Most of all, we hope it will be thought provoking, bringing a competitive edge to management thinking which few organisations have yet achieved.

Most of the text is relevant to any organisation. We do not believe that there is any aspect of a business or service, which has not been directly or implicitly covered. We would welcome suggestions or comments. Whatever else, we are certain it will pay for itself thousands of times over, through saved premiums and more efficient management in all organisations - whether in the corporate or public sectors.

By reading this book alone, you will:
➤ become more aware and in control of your corporate destiny;
➤ make informed choices;
➤ be aware of the challenges and possibilities; and
➤ arrive at optimal risk/reward decisions, leading to sustainable long-term value.

You do not need to read the whole of it to derive this value. The more technical aspects are kept to the end, but even these are presented in simple language, concepts and terms.

## A Template Approach

In Appendix 2, you will find an outline Strategic Business Plan, annotated with questions about managing risk. In Appendix 3, there is a standard template for use in any decision making process. These are the starting point for our proposed approach to the management of strategic and operational choice in your organisation. The other major tool is the 'Template' style, which is adopted throughout the book. This is the basis for *The Risk Factor*.

Like all sound, objective management, the key is in questions. In our experience, the core skill of any Director, MD, CEO or FD, is being able to ask the right questions and not taking rubbish for an answer. Patient, constructive, informed, supportive probing encourages empowered managers to 'raise their heads above the parapet', create and add sustainable net business value. The risk-aware pursuit of informed choices to deliver rewards is more creative and enhancing than cost/benefit analysis.

If every manager in the next millennium will need to be a financial manager, then they should also be managers of risk. Whether or not burgeoning regulation, dictated by management and corporate incompetence leads to the institutionalisation of the management of risk, the innovative, creative, flexible and adaptable manager of tomorrow will see business as a series of choices exercised in the awareness of possible consequences, rather than a series of events beset by threats, policed by a costly regulatory structure.

➤      ➤      ➤

All of the appendices in *The Risk Factor*, plus a number of other useful templates can be downloaded in larger format from www.TheRiskFactor.com

# 4

# Risk and the Corporate Mind

We live in an age where the mind/body connection has become widely accepted. We now also recognise the difference between the mind and brain. The mind is more closely connected with spirituality, free will, emotions and the unconscious patterns of life.

The brain has been compared to a sophisticated central processor. Indeed, some have said that the processing power of the human brain is greater than the sum of all the computing power on earth. How long this will prevail with the growth in biotechnology is hard to predict. Used appropriately, such developments can augment our existing capabilities and replace the routine.

Biogenetics and biotechnology are also transforming the prospects for the human body. Isn't it interesting to compare how far corporations and organisations have come since the advent of mass technology? In addition, the science of management is less than a century old. We should not in any sense under-estimate the enormous gains we have achieved nor the commensurate problems we have created as a result.

We have lived in an age of science for a long time. It may now be time to combine the best of science with the best of art. Technology has become so sophisticated that it can run much of our lives and yet most of us cannot programme the video without referring to the instruction book. Cars are run by computers and it is no longer sufficient to understand the mechanics alone.

If we are really clever and we put genetics to the most appropriate and ethical uses, we can have technology take over the routines of our lives so that we can at last move towards fulfilling our immense potential as a human race.

Now this is a useful metaphor for organisations also. Hammer and Champey wrote about business process reengineering. Some people deliberately or unthinkingly used this as a basis for downsizing. We, on the other hand, see the fundamental review of management and business processes as the cornerstone of reinventing the corporation and the bedrock of continuous improvement.

In making the best use of technology we may sometimes have lost sight of the importance of the key Risk Factor of all, that is, the people. In 1998, in a study by Sheffield University of over 250 companies, HR was found to be at least twice as important as any other strategic factor in the success of the corporation. Company accounts regularly pronounce "our people are our most important asset" and then proceed to pay lip service to the statement.

Even in an age of home working and disaggregation of the corporation, with individuals being encouraged to take responsibility for their own lives and personal development, leading edge organisations are recognising the key importance of being able to attract and keep good people, whatever their relationship to the corporation.

### The Corporate Mind/Body Connection

Once, we might have thought of a corporate mind as being the top team. It is now sensible to see it as being related to the whole organisation. Much management research has gone into the topics of corporate values and corporate culture. In an individual these are equivalent to personal values, attitudes and beliefs. Failing to understand the power of these concepts in the organisation, with their attendant risks, may under-estimate, inhibit or even damage the corporate potential.

The body of the organisation consists of its resources and infrastructure. The brain can be likened to the processes and systems.

Mission, vision, values, brand, motivation, morale and corporate culture may be more closely linked with the corporate mind.

Our right-brain approach to risk management involves all of these elements. Plan for, understand and manage the tangible and physical threats to the corporate body. Some of these may typically involve insurance. Review, redesign and optimise the management and business processes and supporting systems. These represent a corporate brain. Planning and thinking in a systematic way can optimise the quality of the processes and minimises the consequences of risk.

In no other handbook on managing risk will you find consideration of perhaps the most critical of all these aspects: the corporate mind. Whatever the sophistication and completeness of your risk management processes and systems, they can be totally undermined by failing to understand the critical importance of the human factor collected together in this corporate mind.

Charismatic leadership has inspired work forces across the world. Kaizen, TQM (Total Quality Management) and the other quality management practices have transformed business success and the corporate culture at the same time. Our approach is to add to these excellent practices the additional dimension of involvement of all the people in ownership and accountability for corporate aspirations and success and the objective management of the associated risks.

### Further Comparison with the Individual

So let's make further comparison with the thought, decision and action processes of the individual, including the hierarchy of beliefs.

How does the individual make decisions? Let's take two points of view: rational and emotional; conscious and unconscious.

It may still not be widely understood that our logical, rational brain originated from an emotional brain. Daniel Goleman, in his book *Emotional Intelligence* (Bloomsbury 1985) discusses this point. Emotional illiteracy can be caused by the amygdala overwhelming the prefrontal cortex. In other words, sometimes-rational logical thoughts can be sabotaged by emotions. The position of the amygdala is close to the brain stem. A rational brain evolved from the prehistoric emotional brain.

In the organisation we may have a very well defined planning, implementation, measurement and control and review infrastructure. How many times in the past has this been over-ridden by the sometimes-irrational decisions of human beings? There may e.g. be a well-planned and managed set of communications processes. Does this mean that corridor conversations and the jungle telegraph don't coexist?

Of paramount importance in the success of an organisation are motivation and morale. Without a healthy level of both, risks will increase, going way beyond the obvious consequences of higher levels of absence, sickness and staff turnover. Sometimes in poorly managed or poorly understood organisations, counter-cultures can sabotage the best management plans.

We are of course talking about leadership, one of the fundamentals of excellence in emotional intelligence according to Goleman. In the 21st century, many of the best organisations will be those which, apart from the ability to reinvent themselves, will be able to collect together and keep a skilled, motivated, synergistic team. In addition, while creating an empowering culture, they will value, recognise and reward people. The highest quality standards and continuous improvement processes will be de rigueur. Finally, they will be comfortable and objective in recognising, managing and exploiting the risks inherent in the business.

Another separation in thought processes, is that between conscious and unconscious. In many senses this is related to the foregoing. Rational, logical thought tends to be associated with the conscious and emotions with the unconscious. Whatever the rational strategies, plans and processes, the success of the organisation will still depend on the corporate culture.

Many organisations have tried to establish or re-establish a desired corporate culture. They have conducted exercises to identify a mission, vision and values. We have participated in such projects ourselves. The top team may invest much time in coming to an agreed set of values. At the end of the day, however, the values prevalent in the organisation will re-establish themselves if they are strong enough and especially if they are in contradiction to the stated or espoused values. This in itself is a major risk.

To take an example, we were working with an organisation with a massive capital project fundamental to its future strategic plans. Huge amounts of money, time and resource were dedicated during two years to the successful achievement of the project goals. There were many risks during and after the process. In the event, the two, which had the greatest effect, were: the failure by management to take the organisation with it; and the absence of integration between the project and the long-term strategic plan.

Indeed, for a long time, management had apparently failed to see how fundamental the project was to all aspects of the strategic plan. Consequently, the processes for managing the project sat alongside the day-to-day organisational processes.

A huge amount of rational, logical planning and implementation activity went into the delivery of the project. Meanwhile, the 'body of the church' was not fully involved in either, merely being expected to carry on their daily routines. As the pressure and workloads arising from the project increased, they impacted more and more on large numbers of people who had not been involved or consulted sufficiently in the project planning process. Middle ranking and some more senior managers started to leave despite the apparent attractions of being part of a success story when the project was completed.

The local conversations and general feeling carried an increasing sense of frustration and even concern as to whether management knew where they were going. In the event, the project completion had to be put back by several months and for those who remained a general and growing sense of dissatisfaction prevailed rather than the expected pleasure of achievement.

The organisation's motivation and direction was set back several years by this experience. Eventually, it ended up having to seek a merger with a large organisation from a position of weakness. Those who did not leave at the time of the merger remained deeply unhappy for some time afterwards.

It is useful and instructive to look at how the individual processes, manages and takes risks. Look at your self for example. Different people think and operate in different ways. Collectively, we try to apply more science to the organisation. We take risks daily, often without thinking.

Most people drive their cars safely. Yet, they may be listening to the radio having a conversation with a friend, looking out at the view and generally thinking of all the things that they have to do, all the time driving without incident. Who's driving the car? Most of the time our unconscious mind is driving the car and this is true of our lives generally. It is said that at any one time we have to deal with up to 2 billion bits of information. It is also said that we can only consciously handle seven plus or minus two. The rest are sifted through processes of distortion, deletion and generalisation.

All the while, we are seeing, assessing, understanding and managing actual or potential risks. We do this both consciously and unconsciously. This is the desired regime for the corporation or organisation. In life, we sometimes avoid risks or even insure against them. When we enter a new situation, we take stock both consciously and unconsciously, make decisions and move forward. Unless we are for some reason temporarily depressed or debilitated, we manage our lives in an objective, positive way. Conscious decisions about risks in due course become internalised, so that we can move forward at a desired pace.

Equally as important as objectivity and harmony between the conscious and unconscious processes of the organisation is achieving congruence between individuals and the corporation. This is the key to empowerment, commitment and willingness to make risk-aware choices.

While awareness of risk should be intuitive, as well as conscious, decisions should be proactive, not passive or negligent. The process starts with mission, culture and business philosophy. Closely connected to the corporate mind will be investor perceptions, customer attitudes and brand, partly based on management's skills, experience and track record, and influenced by capacity for and judgement of risk.

Every corporation or organisation has responsibilities to its owners, people, customers, suppliers, the general public and other interested parties. A key part of that responsibility is understanding and managing risks.

When you were two, you knew nothing about driving a car - you were unconsciously incompetent. When you first sat in a car with the intention of learning to drive, you were consciously incompetent to drive. When you passed your test and the examiner was prepared to let you out on the roads on your own, you were consciously competent. Now, having driven for some time you can drive safely, all the while doing many other things, because you are unconsciously competent to drive. This is the process by which we learn to do anything, from walking to a new skill.

The same process can be used to create the understanding and objective management of risk in any business or organisation. Breaking into the management of business risk can be difficult - as difficult as you want to make it. As with any process in which you want to involve the whole organisation, it is worthwhile engaging everyone in the way that is most appropriate for them. Risk has had negative connotations in the past. The whole of this book is set in a positive context because that is the way to produce winners in the 21st century.

Managing risk is an important function in all organisations but especially large corporations that have begun to appreciate the impact losses can have on their profits. Maybe in the past it has seemed simpler to pay away risks. In these days of narrowing margins and fleeting markets, it is important for every penny to work for itself. Organisations can no longer afford the unquestioning payment of insurance premiums, not just because of cost but also because they may be missing an opportunity.

So, before reaching for your cheque book to pay those insurance premiums it makes sense to analyse the risks that may affect the business of your organisation and encourage everyone towards the conscious and unconscious recognition and management of risks. Of course, some risks have to be insured if the organisation is to meet its legal obligations and it makes sense to insure some others from a sound financial point of view. The key here is objectivity and opportunity.

### Applying the Corporate Mind to Risk

Earlier, we had a definition of risk. In defining the management of risk, we may also consider what it is not. Historically, risk has tended to be treated in a negative context. We have proposed that it should be managed in a positive context, opportunistically. Although initially an organisation will want to spend time understanding risk and its optimum management, ultimately our aim is for it to become embedded in the management and business processes.

In the past, organisations have tended to set up a function for the management of risk. While this may be entirely appropriate for a bank for example, or a similar financial services institution, we do not propose in the long run a department for managing risk in most organisations. In other words, risk is so fundamental to the planning and implementation processes of every organisation that it should be an inextricable part of daily corporate life. Consciously, or unconsciously, the corporate mind should be alert to and, where appropriate, aware of the risk consequences of every action that they take.

Our own treatment of the management of risk is different from and entirely separate from risk control. So what does the subject include? There are several textbooks you could consult in understanding the basic elements of traditional management of risk. We propose to go beyond that. Our intention is not to instruct, but to elicit, empower and encourage intuitive and insightful thinking about risk throughout the organisation.

The first challenge, therefore, is that of defining what is 'it' that the management of risk includes? Unfortunately the skill of managing risk is generally made too complicated or confusing and consequently it does not deliver the promised benefits.

*The Risk Factor* aims to make the managing of risk transparent to the reader and, ideally to most people in the organisation, by:

> Explaining why risk needs to be managed;
> Why management of risk is essential to all business decisions;
> Highlighting the hidden cost of risk;
> Showing how risk management is often approached as a number of one-offs;
> Showing how you can seize opportunities and control the threats;
> Explaining why the balance of risk and reward is fundamental to achieving organisational profitability or other objectives;
> Proposing key headings to enable a structure to be clearly established within a business or organisation;
> Identifying key roles, tasks and scheduling;
> Establishing an idea of what is best practice.

This book will assist the reader by:

> Providing a greater understanding and appreciation of the subject
> Enabling a recognition of the extent of the subject (including the global extent of the subject matter);
> Enabling the completion of a 'snapshot' of the business or organisation's progress towards its management of risk;
> Creating links to Corporate Governance, Audit and Accountability - bringing them together in a sound, integrated system for business risk assessment;
> Identifying and encouraging the business's (or organisation's) appetite for risk;

In passing, we would ask the question whether risk tolerance is understood, shared and acted upon by ALL those within your organisation whose actions continually impact on the organisation's performance ?

The current point reached in the organisation or corporation's progress is set in the context of the strategic or business plan. It is a combination of the opportunities and risks inherent in the current state. We need a method and a process whereby we can assess the current position accurately and objectively so that we can create a strategy for improving performance while understanding and optimising risk.

The organisation will also need to understand how to get help, when it might be needed and what should be expected. There are many different approaches, not least the management of risk approach based on traditional insurance methods. This has a limited perspective for dealing with the risks you wish to divert. The question is how do you reach the point when you have decided this, let alone understanding and managing the other risks that are present.

### The Role of the Board and Management

The role of the Board is critical in optimising the management of risk for the organisation's benefit. Cadbury and Hampel may have generated a negative mindset in some organisations, one of regulation and compliance. Whichever way one looks at it, the implications are regressive.

If risk control and compliance have been imposed from outside or on the recommendation or insistence of the auditors or some other external authority, then the implication is that the organisation has lost some of its initiative and direction. Some organisations are much better than this, of course, seeing the need or the value of compliance and/or structured management of risk before it is recommended or imposed from outside. If, however, they follow the processes slavishly, they may be spending too much money on either the processes or insurance itself, as well as missing the wider opportunities of self-determination.

There is a role for the wider organisation in managing risk. We can even link it to competitive advantage (or disadvantage). An equation can be created which relates the current cost to the current value of managing risk in the business. What we are aiming to achieve here is preventing managing risk from becoming just another administrative burden, probably resented by many within the business. In doing so, one of our aims is to help the organisation to produce a users guide or action pack, usable by everybody who is relevant or involved.

As we have mentioned earlier, this book starts the process by providing useable templates. Its approach is to create something that can be shared with others and that can be dipped into when it is recognised that the business has a need to 'get back on track'.

The main body of the subject has been broken into eight chapters representing a suggested number of key tasks that need to be addressed.

We have talked of definitions earlier. One of the first issues to be addressed is of terminology. This means attributing a global meaning to the words that the business wants to be associated with the subject. These can be used within the business, knowing that everyone involved recognises not only the words but also the meaning that the business ascribes to them.

### The Eight Core Elements of Risk Factor Based Management
1. Risk Strategy
2. Risk (Action) Planning
3. Risk Information Flow
4. Risk Education (& Training)
5. Risk (Process) Structure
6. Risk Recording
7. Risk Handling
8. Risk Assurance (Audit & Compliance)

### The Key Risk Factors
The key Risk Factor areas in any business organisation can be grouped as follows:
A. Financial Implications
B. Decision Making
C. Process & Structure

D.   People (& Machines)
E.   Legal and Regulatory Requirements
F.   Customers/Client Needs
G.   Environmental Considerations
H.   Communication Requirements

## A. Financial Implications

These can of course be both positive and negative. They include the following:

➤   The numbers themselves;

➤   The analysis of the numbers; and

➤   The interpretation of that analysis.

Taking the wider picture we can include:

a)   The economic outlook;

b)   Predictions, forecasts and scenarios;

c)   The actual or expected incidence of fraud, dishonesty, theft or misappropriation;

d)   The need for bonds or fidelity guarantees;

e)   Swaps, derivatives and other financial engineering or balance sheet management tools;

f)   Ways of valuing the enterprise;

g)   Methods of valuing and managing assets;

h)   And the implications of any or all of the above and other factors on the share price (where relevant);

## B. Decision Making

a)   The process for, and quality of, business decisions - how are they made;

b)   Equating good decisions with those that produce benefits or limit or prevent loss of value;

c)   Defining your decisions in terms of those that cause damage or inhibit the achievement of objectives;

d)   Relevance of business decisions;

e)   Priority and weighting in business decisions;

f)   Timing of business decisions including when to delay them or not make them at all;

g)   Weighting; and

h)   The extent to which empowerment is assisting

## C.  Process & Structure

This includes:

a)   How risk is being managed;

b)   How risk is integrated into the broader management processes;

c)   What people do in the context of managing risk;

d)   Identified responsibilities for specific individuals;

e)   The appropriateness of feedback mechanisms

f)   The two way communication processes;

g)   Recognition of expectations from within the organisation; and

h)   Active to recognise external expectations.

## D.  People (& Machines)

This includes:

a)   Who does what;

b)   Which people lead and are involved;

c)   The risks inherent in employment;

d)   The recruitment process and the initiatives for motivation and retention;

e)   Procedures for dismissal and/or redundancy;

f)   Employment legislation and best practice;

g)   Use of and accountability for machines; and

h)   Security and accountability; etc.

## E.  Legal and Regulatory Requirements

This includes:

a)   What to comply with?

b)   Are we complying in this country?

c)   Are we complying where we sell goods or deliver services?

d)   Who is responsible?

e)   Who is accountable?

f)   Turnbull - what is happening?
g)   Corporate Governance - where are we?
h)   What changes are on the horizon?

## F. Customers/Clients

This includes:

a)   Changing standards;
b)   Changing needs;
c)   Fads - changing markets;
d)   The ability to deliver their part of the deal;
e)   Reputations;
f)   Losing customers/clients;
g)   Handling unexpected business (e.g. recent ecommerce activity); and
h)   The effects of competition.

## G. Environmental Considerations

This includes:

a)   Political;
b)   Economic;
c)   Global;
d)   Industry;
e)   Sectoral;
f)   Market;
g)   Community and public at large; and
h)   The surrounding and further afield environmental issues.

## H. Communication Requirements

This includes:

a)   Are we clearly defining what we mean by risk?
b)   Are risk issues being clearly recognised?
c)   Are the relevant parties talking the same language?
d)   How wide is the involvement and understanding?
e)   Has the 'message' been defined?
f)   Is 'the message' being communicated to relevant parties?
g)   How do we handle the media when things go wrong? And
h)   What message do we give our customers, suppliers and stakeholders when things don't go to plan?

### A Structured Approach to Managing Risk

We now come to the main body of this text. All sound business and organisation management commences with strategy. Having considered the strategic Risk Factor and all its aspects we then move to implementation. The latter section represents the core of our approach. It has eight main elements, discussed earlier:

> Risk Strategy, including integration with the organisation's strategic direction;

> Risk (Action) Planning, including integration with the tactical business planning process.

> Risk Information Flow, including obtaining timely and relevant information throughout the organisation.

> Risk Education (&Training), including risk simulation training to promote awareness of the organisations risk handling activity.

> Risk (Process) Structure, including ensuring that the business structure is designed to actually deliver successful risk handling processes.

> Risk Recording, including the most appropriate collection and storage relevant information that will aid the decision making process on the handling of risk.

> Risk Handling, including the decision making process, should risk be retained within the business or transferred to third parties and how risk is to be handled when things don't go according to plan.

> Risk Assurance (Audit & Compliance), including integrating the process of assurance when designing the systems and learning the lessons from the effect of risk in and on the organisation.

**Appendix 1** is the key template in the Risk Factor questionnaire. It poses the question "how are we doing?" The matrix maps the eight main elements above against the eight key Risk Factors. Further explanation as to how to use the appendix is in the relevant section at the end of the book.

>      >      >

# PART B

# The Strategic
# Risk Factor

# 5

# Risk and Corporate Strategy

Do you invest in stocks and shares? If so, you'll probably develop a pile of prospectuses and annual reports similar to ours. Pulling one out of the stack at random, it was found to be placing an open offer for new shares in a company that manufactures retractable syringes. The idea is good and there is a ready and growing market in the US. Needle stick injuries are part of a continuing clinical Risk Factor in the Health Service. Unfortunately, development, production, marketing and delivery had taken much longer than expected and the company had run dangerously low on funds (part of a continuing financial Risk Factor). Accordingly, they had come to the market for a further £20 million.

I mention this, because the prospectus included a section headed 'Risk Factors'. It warned that prospective investors should be aware that an investment in the Company involved a higher than normal degree of risk. A list followed which did not claim to be exhaustive, or to summarise all the risks which might be pertinent, pointing out that there might be other risks associated with making an investment in the Company.

The Risk Factors listed are: performance; stage of development; manufacturing; competition; retention of patents and proprietary rights; product liability and insurance; history of operating losses and accumulated deficit.

Risk is an accepted fact of daily life in corporate management. It is now standard practise to include an assessment of Risk Factors in documents such as the one mentioned above. What is more important is that the management and business processes for any organisation should include intrinsic instinctive risk management. As with the best management practice this starts with the strategic plan.

## Strategic Planning and Managing Risk

"Business risk arises as much from the likelihood that something good *won't* happen as it does from the threat that something bad *will* happen." (The Economist Intelligence Unit, *Managing Business Risks: An Integrated Approach,* 1995).

"The strategist's method is very simply to challenge the prevailing assumptions with a single question: Why? and to put the same question relentlessly to those responsible for the current way of doing things until they are sick of it." (Kenichi Ohmae, *The Mind of the Strategist,* McGraw Hill, 1982).

Strategic planning has been around for over 30 years. In 1965, Igor Ansoff, to many the father of strategic planning, wrote *Corporate Strategy,* the first definitive book on the subject. In the UK, thinking took a major step forward in 1968, with the publication of *Corporate Planning: A Practical Guide* (Allen & Unwin). In recent years, it has been Michael Porter who has been the most influential long-term influence, particularly in his work on competitive advantage in markets. As a professor at Harvard Business School, he pioneered thinking on *Competitive Strategy* in 1980, at a time when it was very much the approach of Boston Consulting Group and McKinseys, which was making organisations take note.

We now live in the age of the guru (e.g. Chris Argyris), but despite this long history, less than 10% of companies in the UK use strategic planning. Some would argue that there isn't time to invest in a medium term plan, let alone long term, when change happens daily. This is to ignore the value of a strategic canvas, comprising mission, vision, values and goals, against which management decisions can be taken.

If we were to make a long journey, would we ignore the route map because of the likelihood that there would be road works in several places on the way? In fact we would not only get a holistic picture of our journey, planning stops on the way, but it would also be available at all times, in order to condition our decisions and change of course when unforeseen challenges intervened. These might also include environmental conditions and the needs of our passengers on the way.

This is to illustrate not only the value of strategic planning as a basis for management action (as well as communication of intent to stakeholders), but also the importance of it being flexible and adaptable and, above all, understandable to all concerned.

The management of risk has an even shorter history in text and academe. It has been pointed out elsewhere that very few business schools teach it and the remainder may undo what little good work has been achieved. As was illustrated earlier, risk is as old as history.

Perhaps in recent times the challenges and threats of business and personal life have conditioned us to take a cautious view of risk. The best way forward for the 21st century must surely be to grasp risk in a positive sense, either as the necessary corollary of increasing opportunities for reward, and/or a series of challenges. If we are aware of them, of a positive frame of mind, prepared to take them on or manage them from the basis of intelligent understanding and objectivity, they must surely yield a competitive advantage along the way.

Risk is inevitable and implicit in everything we do. If we try to avoid it we shall achieve nothing. If we try to wholly neutralise it, the costs will outweigh any residual rewards.

The understanding of risk starts with The Risk Factor in strategic planning. The culture we want to create however is not one of worrying about the negatives and constraining the innovation, creativity, initiative and competitiveness of the organisation. We do not want convoluted structures for managing risk, or the finance department telling us what we can't do and why at every stage. We want managers and employees who are challenging from an objective viewpoint, managing with an awareness of risks, knowing instinctively that rewards will outweigh both the costs and the consequences of decisions. No, this is not speculation, it is entrepreneurship.

While there are many non-entrepreneurial situations and decisions to be made in the daily life of a company, The Risk Factor advocates an entrepreneurial, informed approach to all such decisions, rather than an administrative, overcautious trudge forward.

The Finance Director can be a major catalyst in the success of this approach. As recommended in *The Role of the Finance Director*, this should be one of advice, guidance, support and facilitation of objective strategic and business management, not financial constraint. By all means, finance can quantify the consequences of decisions, but the information needs to be available in real-time, should include best, worst and most likely scenarios (Tmax, Tmin and Tsat, in Argenti's equivalents), revenues and costs, in order that management can make informed choices.

The strategic 'template' in Appendix 3, is a series of questions. We do not wish, as in olden times, to lay down a formulaic approach to strategic planning or thinking. The organisation does not need to slavishly follow the questions proposed. It is the approach, which is important, questioning everything from an objective viewpoint, but seeing a series of challenges and opportunities where reward outweighs costs and risks, rather than a series of roadblocks, which slow down the journey or might lead to it being abandoned. Where strategic analysis leads to the cessation of significant activity, it should only be where the net long-term value added would be greater than if it was continued, or better still where there is a more attractive opportunity(ies).

The above sets the strategic management of risk clearly in the context of challenge, opportunity and choice, as opposed to risk, threat, obstacle, negativity, shrinking enterprise or even abandonment. We are in a time now, when companies are narrowing down corporate strategy and enterprise, declining investment, selling off or closing down operations and paying back capital to investors. While this may avoid the possibility of increasing risk, it also reduces the possibility of improving rewards.

Is it really in the interests of creating long-term value for shareholders when, by definition, if more corporations adopt this approach, more funds will be left in shareholders' hands, chasing a shrinking number of opportunities and therefore diminishing total returns? If debt is accepted to be cheaper than equity, then compelling investors to fixed returns must reduce their long-term value creation.

This is the result of the unadventurous, non-strategic, tactical management, which has characterised the UK for too long. In truth, the 'cult of the amateur' is still prevalent. Where it is adventurous it has too often indulged in blind speculation, leading to spectacular failure, with the natural bureaucratic response of stiffening regulation. Where it is unadventurous, the returns are minuscule compared with those that are consistently achieved in the US and were the hallmark of Japanese economic progress since the war.

If this book were to be mould-breaking, it would seek to achieve a complete change in the UK management mindset. The consequence of wholesale redundancy in the 1980s is that legions of 20 and 30-something managers are coming through. What legacy do we want to leave them - caution and regulation, or entrepreneurship and innovation? If they are persuaded to opt for the former, who on earth will pay our pensions, as specific and overall economic returns decline in real terms, while the working population declines and the overall population ages?

Make no mistake, this book is about managing risk, but it is about making risk work for you. It is about the holistic management of choice, based on an integrated understanding of all the opportunities and threats, strengths and weaknesses, which face any enterprise. The Risk Factor starts and ends with people. People understand risk and opportunity. People make informed choices, in the expectation that return will exceed cost and risk in the long term. When the unforeseen intervenes, people re-examine strategy and choices, make the necessary corrections and move on, once more confident that they are generating incremental long-term value.

## The Strategic Planning Process

Risk is inherent in an entrepreneurial strategic plan. The Risk Factor is about understanding risk in order to optimise the balance between risk and reward, thereby generating incremental value and, where appropriate, acting to protect that value.

A popular and successful approach to equity investment involves buying shares, setting a stop-loss level at a fixed percentage below the share price as it moves up and effecting a sale when the price falls by that fixed percentage. Ideally, when the share price doubles in value, half the shares are sold, to leave the remainder, equivalent to the original value of purchase, effectively 'free of cost'.

Whilst not being a direct analogy, this is an effective metaphor for entrepreneurial management of risk. Secure possible losses in a foreseen set of circumstances, progressively enhance value in a risk-aware frame of mind and act to secure rewards in appropriate circumstances, thereby releasing capital to invest in developing or broadening the portfolio.

Funds run for 'widows and orphans' may achieve safe, unspectacular returns through cautious investment. The investor who leaves their money on the sidelines may miss both the ups and downs of the market and the cash value may be secured, but history shows that over any five year period since the war, the real returns will be much lower than those achieved by investing in enterprise through shares. That is why funds and shareholders invest and that is what they expect management to achieve.

## Using the Strategic Template

The Strategic Planning Template in Appendix 2 is an outline strategic planning process, with annotated questions relating to risks, consequences, challenges and choices. It is designed to be the basis of a flexible, adaptable, evolving, strategic planning process. While it might be adopted for an annual exercise, it would also form the basis for monthly Board and weekly senior management meetings. It is the framework against which performance is reviewed and challenged and strategic and operational decisions are reviewed, challenged and revised.

Management would review the strategic direction weekly. This does not mean that they would consider all of the questions below, every week. A senior manager would facilitate the process with responsibility for designing and implementing the planning process. Reporting direct to the CEO/MD, who leads the process, this role might be combined into that of FD in smaller organisations.

Whoever holds the planning brief, their responsibility is to be in constant dialogue with all the key decision makers in the organisation, who will be aware of all of these questions, especially in relation to the specific management processes they lead. The planner would consider all of these matters in detail at least once a year and implicitly on an ongoing basis, in order to inform the top team.

The top team will delegate as much of the day-to-day management of processes as possible, so that they can preoccupy themselves with how the business is performing against the agreed strategic direction, goals, objectives and key performance indicators. Any significant variances would be considered in conjunction with the planner and FD, in order to determine whether there is a need to reconsider or vary the overall strategic direction, or any key decisions.

It is important to understand that this strategic planning process should be slick and efficient, not strangle the business leadership with administration and bureaucracy. The role of the top team is not to make every decision in the organisation, but to agree the overall, evolving, strategic direction, communicate it to empowered teams to implement (involving them in the consideration process and constantly seeking feedback), making changes where appropriate.

The overall strategic direction and any significant revisions would be discussed with and recommended to the Board at a monthly meeting. The Board would have a copy of all the strategic questions and challenges and would expect management to have anticipated the possible challenges. You will note that the word risk does not appear often in what follows.

The objective, forward-thinking, flexible, adaptable, empowering organisation will implicitly or explicitly consider the risk consequences of every decision it makes, but will see these as opportunities or challenges. The expectation would be that in a reward/risk-oriented culture, business management would consider risk at every stage, rather than have a separate bureaucracy and structure for the management of risk. The successful business of the 21st century cannot afford to be strangled by regulation, procedure and bureaucracy.

In a large organisation, there might, however, be a risk manager, who would be a member of the top team, working closely with the FD, planner and auditor. Their wide contact with the organisation makeup and skills would help the organisation to understand and anticipate risk, as well as make the optimum decisions as to how to manage, protect against or insure the risks identified. In a smaller organisation, the risk manager's role, if it exists separately, would be combined into either the FD or the auditor's role (who in any case should adopt a risk-aware, internal consultancy style, helping the business to better understand the risk consequences of its decisions and the best ways to manage them to optimise the reward/risk trade-off).

The daily management of business processes would be enhanced by use of the template in Appendix 3, as a basis to ensure that risk-aware decisions are made, once again to maximise profitability at a planned and managed level of risk. Removing or insulating against all risk by definition implies the removal or neutralisation of profit opportunities. Indeed, the cost of insurance (whether through underwriting or use of derivatives) inevitably means that to insure against all risks means running at a loss.

### Risk, Reward and Strategic Choice

It has been traditional to see a trade-off between risk and reward. It is certainly true that the management of any organisation or enterprise implies a degree of risk by its very existence. The question in the past has often been what degree of risk to stand, in pursuit of the desired reward.

Even if risk is implicit in everything we do, our preference is to recognise the fact and make risk work for you rather than to nail whole chunks down or pay away the cost of parts we don't want to worry about in insurance premiums. To put it another way, we are talking about understanding every aspect of the business or organisation, making sure every decision is deliberate and informed and seeing virtually all risks as opportunities.

Let's consider this for a moment. Even with a purposeful planned and structured organisation or business, with clearly defined goals and objectives, there are risks in everything you do. What we recommend is that you understand these from the outset as part of your planning consideration. It has often been the practise in the past in many organisations to pay insurance premiums or even avoid (deliberately or through ignorance) the raft of risks that they didn't have the time or inclination to consider.

Apart from the fact that our experience has shown that the relatively indiscriminate payment of insurance premiums can be financially wasteful, it misses the opportunity to better understand the business in a way that even now many of your competitors may not be doing. And it starts with strategic planning.

We advocate a holistic management approach, looking at the business organisation in its entirety through from planning to implementation, measurement and control and review for continuous quality improvement. Many may see this as a potentially time-consuming process. Our experience over and over again is that the investment of time, not only in the planning process but also in the day-to-day implementation routine, pays dividends in terms not only of saved expenditure but also in improved opportunity, profitability or service efficiency.

Managing risk is not just about protecting value, it is also about enhancing value for owners. Will Hutton, in his book 'The State We're In' (Vintage, 1996) eloquently captured the concept of a stakeholder society and economy. As you will find in the present text we also embrace a wider definition of the stakeholder and we are talking about both enterprise and service organisation in the corporate and public sectors. The concept of stakeholder is readily transportable across all sectors and provides a common currency.

So what are stakeholder interests? In the corporate sector they imply profit maximisation and loss or cost minimisation. But they also go wider than this. Traditionally, and still very much in the statements in annual reports, etc. the management of enterprise is aimed at creating and increasing long-term shareholder value. Whether imposed by political, regulatory or other factors, expressed or implied through wider public pressures, there is a growing agenda of stakeholder values.

Brand has become the prime medium through which many of these have been captured. We shall discuss brand at greater length elsewhere, but as the Union Carbide case demonstrated, pursuit of financial goals at the expense of consideration of broader factors such as the environment can damage the ability to earn profits much more than the profits themselves.

So the implication here is that risk evaluation should be incorporated into every stage of the strategic planning process itself.

## The Corporate Planning Process

The key elements in corporate planning are: direction, resources, implementation, measurement, and improvement. We cannot over stress the importance of a corporate planning process aimed at achieving the optimum: balancing the corporate strategy with the most favourable integration of the resources of people, processes and systems. Above all this implies the need for a coherent, holistic risk strategy.

### Competitive Strategy and Managing Risk

We live in an age where innovation is of paramount importance. Every aspect of innovation implies risk. But where would most of the successful enterprises in the world have been without innovating in a conscious context of risk. How else can market leadership be achieved and sustained without innovation. What we are talking about here is going beyond this point and achieving a further edge by differentiation through a risk positive-approach to the enterprise.

Brand and reputation are fundamental here. Successful innovation and enterprise will lead to enhanced brand image. Lack of success, mistake or failure and inadequacy in achieving potential could result in deterioration of brand or reputation. Whilst PR and advertising are important we would want them to be used to positively enhance brand rather than to pick up the pieces when things go wrong. Of course we shall never be able to anticipate everything but we can dramatically improve our foresight and therefore our success by integrating an understanding of risk into the planning and management processes.

Finally, there is a need to consider intellectual property right (IPR). One only needs to look at the astonishing development of the Internet and all its associated products and services, or even the scramble to decode the genome and capitalise on the genetic opportunities to understand the importance of IPR.

Every commercial enterprise has intangible aspects to protect that often go beyond just the corporate or product names. In a multitude of areas of both the corporate and public sectors, IPR is being created or discovered daily. Failure to understand what you already have or are capable of developing before others do so could result in missed opportunities, or worse still deterioration or loss of the key intangibles on which the business is founded.

A somewhat banal example is the registration of domain names. Many well-known corporations and other organisations have found that they have either had to pay substantial amounts of money to acquire the critical domain names to express their identity, or they have had to make do with an inferior alternative. This has come about because of an industry of private individuals and corporations making a business of spotting or inventing domain name opportunities.

The risk here can be expressed in one of three ways: the cost of acquiring the domain name; the loss of potential in having to settle for an inferior name; the potential loss of brand recognition or at least confusion where another organisation is able to use a similar identity in the rapidly growing global markets based around the Internet.

### External Factors

Many external factors are discussed in part D, but suffice to say, here, that every strategic planning process requires a consideration of such factors including again, the opportunities and risks. Shell's scenario planning in the 1960's is again a very good example of how to invest time and resource in protecting long-term value. In western society, governments usually change every four or five years. Even when the same party is re-elected the period before the election date is usually characterised by proposed new policies or policy changes captured in an election manifesto.

As someone once put it, governments will typically spend the first two years in office implementing manifesto promises and the second two years preparing for the next election. Apart from the potential destabilisation of the economy and markets, new legislation invariably has a direct or indirect impact on corporate organisational planning or policy. We cannot normally expect corporations or organisations to anticipate what is in the minds of the political parties or the future. However, any strategic planning process that fails to take account of what is already in the public domain is implicitly increasing the risks to the organisation.

Competition is the most significant external factor of all. If it is difficult to predict political change and consequences, it is becoming even more so for market and product change. There are two saving graces however. First, the rapid pace of change in technology has dramatically reduced the response times to competitive change. Second, while fashion has become more flexible, the use of demographic, opinion polls, focus groups and an understanding of the power of the media can for many organisations impact their ability to understand, plan for and manage competitive risks.

These steps may not be able to prevent the advent of a major market decline. This is one of the reasons why the ability to continually reinvent the corporation is of paramount importance. There are a growing number of public companies, whose business is based on traditional products, which are having to face the prospect of continually downsizing their enterprise or even, ultimately, winding up or disposing of the business and repaying capital to investors.

This again brings us back to the importance of brand. As Marlborough has shown, a decline in tobacco consumption in western markets can be compensated by transporting the brand to other very different products and markets. Diversification is another very useful strategy.

The strategic planning process does not have to capture the external and internal risks, as many will emerge and be managed through the daily management processes. It should certainly however capture the key corporate risks. It should also be the precursor to setting corporate risk policies.

## *Managing Risk as Internal Consultancy*

If there is to be a risk function, the time has come for the management of risk to be established as an internal consultancy. When we initially introduced the concept in N&P (a major UK financial services organisation), it was a specific function. Managing risk was in its infancy in 1986. The first purpose was to broaden the awareness and understanding of risk in the organisation. As a major financial services provider, it was wise to consider financial risk in every aspect of our product considerations.

Our intention in introducing a function for managing risk was to go beyond financial risk. Having had a recommended approach accepted by the Board, we produced an internal document to help the understanding of what we planned. The risk function then worked with every department of the organisation to facilitate the production of a risk manual, which ensured that we considered risk and managed for it optimally in every aspect of the management and business processes.

Risk soon became a way of life. The next stage was to integrate the functions of audit and management of risk into an internal consultancy whose purpose was to help protect value but also to identify and capture the learning opportunities, which could help us to create and sustain long-term value. So, risk became opportunity and although for other reasons N&P eventually became part of Abbey National, this pioneering approach very much set the seal in our understanding and approach to objective, holistic, empowering management of risk.

➤     ➤     ➤

# 6

# Corporate Business Risk

The purpose of managing holistic business risk is to protect and augment long-term shareholder value. The corporate objective should be to optimise the total return on the balance sheet, at a managed level of risk. In the public sector the objective might be to ensure the means to deliver a sustainable service at a managed level of risk. This is the essence of Asset/Liability management, which originated in the US, is captured in many other texts and has been around for many years.

Asset/liability management begins with an understanding of the nature and duration of the assets and liabilities in the business. The optimal aim is to balance the equation of maximising the return on assets, minimising the cost of liabilities, maximising the exploitation opportunity, recognising and understanding risk and making it work for you.

Although some might find it easier to describe it in a different way, corporate business risk also exists in the public and voluntary sectors. It is, in effect, a collation of all the risks to the success, sustainability, viability and long-term value of the enterprise or organisation. For corporate enterprise risk has been magnified by the consequences of globalisation. Globalisation also offers many opportunities for the aware, adaptable and enterprising organisation.

In considering adaptability, let's pause for a moment and consider Year 2000 (or Y2K). For some time before the advent of the millennium, there had been a dichotomy between those who warned against the worst consequences and those who felt that the whole exercise had been overblown. We shall never know. What is certain is that many advantages and benefits accrued from the exercise.

Organisations gained a better and holistic understanding of their business. Systems were reviewed and thoroughly overhauled, being replaced where necessary. In many cases, this forced or allowed a move to the next generation of computing. Old, outdated software was replaced with new. Investment plans were advanced. A better understanding of management and business processes was a widespread benefit.

By definition, the Y2K exercise was an exercise in risk management. Above all, organisations and their people, while greatly inconvenienced by the contingency arrangements for the New Year, were able to discover how much 'stretch' there was in the business. This will be of inestimable value in the increasingly competitive and demanding business life.

## *Practical Business Risk*

At this stage, as an instructive exercise, why not write down an exhaustive list of all types of risk that you feel that are relevant to your business or organisation. By all means use the Pareto approach, but we believe it is worthwhile investing fifteen or 20 minutes of your time now.

So what did you come up with? Later in this chapter is a list of strategic and operational risks. In itself this is not exhaustive, but then the whole of our approach in this book is to encourage structured, original thought, which we believe will result in better understanding and ownership of the risks in your organisation. There is also a more practical consideration of risk in part D.

So let's just consider review. Take new business risk. We could consider two key aspects: the risk of engaging in new or extended business; and the risks that new business will not be achievable and sustainable in the future. Have you considered the consequences of these?

Industrial espionage has been around for some considerable time. The Volkswagen case is a very public and expensive example of the potential consequences of such an approach. While recognising that you would not use such methods in your own business, industrial espionage takes many forms. Beyond the historical example of breaking in to steal your company secrets, there are many other and sometimes more sinister possibilities.

E.g., how effective are the firewalls in your computer systems (assuming you have them)? If teenagers can hack into the Pentagon's computer systems then how many people can breach your own system security and how much of the value of your business is contained therein?

Another example, very relevant in the Volkswagen case, is the situation where an ex-employee takes your secrets to a competitive organisation. While you may be able to use the legal system to prevent the public exploitation of your competitive advantage, how will you know whether your design and development ideas are being incorporated into competitive products? Maybe not at all until they emerge in the marketplace. And litigation itself, apart from being potentially very expensive has also been shown in some cases to damage the brand of an organisation.

Fraud and malice also go beyond the mundane misappropriation and theft. In one case we came across in the public sector, a crusading whistleblower that felt he had been unreasonably dismissed wreaked his vengeance on his former employer by being interviewed in the media about very embarrassing disclosures involving the abuse of research projects. Although this was a public sector organisation it still had a brand and image in the public eye. The negative publicity had an adverse impact on perceptions in the community at large.

## Core Business Risk.

In considering corporate business risk, one key question is about what it actually is? By core business risk, we mean the risk or risks, which are fundamental to the continuation of the business. There are two aspects here: what is fundamental to the business's existence; and what is fundamental to its continuing enterprise.

In this book we do not specifically consider the Risk Factor in marketing and operations. This is a topic, which could occupy a book on its own. Instead, our approach here is to encourage or stimulate you, the business, organisation, director or manager to ask the right questions and keep on asking them until objective management of risk has become part of the very fabric of your organisation.

To consider just a few examples however, there are obviously risks in business development, concentration, new ventures and new products. The demand to develop new products and get them to the marketplace as quickly as possible does not always allow for such considerations. And there is the technical risk inherent in many products. It may be considered that these are largely covered by the engineering and quality management processes. But we are not just talking here about the engineering of the product.

Take the example of the manufacturer of retractable syringes, given earlier. Its intellectual property, concept, and product design were an excellent example of the potential for creating and exploiting new ideas and new markets. Indeed, beyond that, it went to the heart of understanding a need and providing the solution for it. Demand for product exceeded all expectations but after a year or more it still hadn't been met. The main reasons were: the product itself was not safe at the required time (partly because of the inadequacies in the supply of components); secondly, they had overlooked the fact that users required to order more than one size of syringe. The company had focussed its energy on the production and distribution of one size.

Logistics has become one of the core functions of modern industry. One of its main areas of relevance in the past had been the supply of goods to supermarkets. With global markets now being based on the Internet, there has been a rapid growth of overnight delivery services to ensure that the product can be delivered almost as rapidly as the competing alternative without delivery costs impacting on the overall price.

Any of you who have bought business or consumer goods through the Internet may have experienced the frustrations when the process fails. The pace of Internet business means that corporate and product brands can be developed almost overnight. They do carry within them however, significant inherent risks. The consumer's expectations are very much higher. Customers can be wooed very quickly. While price is a key determinant, if or when the service falls down a customer may be lost for all time maybe having only just arrived. Furthermore, the old adage is that a customer tells an average of two people about good service and an average of ten people about bad service.

So if distribution risk and logistics have become a key factor, there is a multiplicity of the other Risk Factors that are new or have changed their character. With the growth of call centre based operations, both for sales and after service, there are whole new aspects of risk. Again, as with the example above, there is the risk of building up customer expectations only for them to be dashed when the support systems and processes fall down. On top of which, at the call centre personnel themselves can become very frustrated when they are operating in a high pressure competitive market and the business processes behind them fail.

Customers may be hard to come by but they are much easier to lose and they often do not come back. Innovation can also be a double-edged sword. How many examples can you think of where a new product has had to be recalled later because of deficiencies or inherent dangers? The problem about the pace of competition is that it encourages the growth of that kind of risk taking as opposed to the informed, aware, holistic approach that we advocate. With whole markets at stake, factors such as product quality, liability and contamination risk, etc. become even more important.

And we do not need to focus just on customers. Suppliers can be the source of as many problems, especially in a just-in-time environment. While economic factors have dictated a massive increase in outsourcing and subcontracting from all over the globe, the remoteness of production for supplying, differing cultures, practices and production standards can be exacerbated by the distance between supply and demand.

This is not in any way forgetting the risks inherent in the customer and supplier transactions themselves. The Internet, credit cards and the growth in global currencies such as the Euro and the dollar, means that consumer goods are increasingly being supplied from all over the globe. The risk to the customer might be in credit card fraud or other financial aspects of the transaction. The corollary for the supplier is not only the risk of losing a customer but also the wider risk to its brand when systems fail. For example, several of the Internet banks have had teething troubles, particularly in relation to dealing with the expected volumes of new customers.

Production systems and processes have their own inherent risks that also will become more complicated as markets become more complex and sophisticated with escalating demand factors. Many may believe that TQM has become 'old hat'. What has in fact happened, is that it has become institutionalised. In the new global markets, highly sophisticated quality, customer service and complaints procedures have become mandatory. Maybe the only saving grace is that labour disputes have become more scarce. This should not in any way undervalue the importance of not taking the workforce for granted. We say again, people are the key Risk Factor.

With more new markets, inexorable growth of enterprise, complementary growth of regulation, continuing demand for new, and new sources of, finance, etc., due diligence, contract and legal documentation risk will remain an important Risk Factor. Directors' liability will also become a more prevalent consideration. Some believe that in the past, directors have often got off lightly, especially where they have been guilty of fraud or misappropriation.

In an ideal world, we should not need regulation and compliance. Self-regulation should be sufficient, but that's not the way it is and we have come too far. There are risks not only in the failure to understand the significance and relevance of regulation, but also in the regulation itself. Meanwhile, the growth of litigation continues apace in every aspect of personal and business life. The object of course is to avoid it in the first place and this requires both practical and intuitive management of risk.

# Strategic/Operational, Entrepreneurial/Non-Entrepreneurial Risk Categories

Below we have listed a number of different types of strategic and operational risk, categorised between entrepreneurial and non-entrepreneurial. This schedule is neither definitive nor exhaustive. It serves merely as a prompt to the thinking or questions that the risk-aware director, executive or manager could be asking.

## Entrepreneurial

| Strategic | Operational |
|---|---|
| Globalisation | Sabotage |
| Catastrophe | Behaviour |
| Marketing Strategy | Fraud |
| Financial Strategy | Product/Process/System Design |
| Investment Strategy | Marketing Implementation |
| Acquisitions Strategy | Manufacture/Production |
| Corporate Reputation/Brand | Logistics/Distribution |
| Consumer Behaviour | Finance |
| Investor Relations | Cash Flow |
| Business Risk | Pricing |
| Financing | Costs |
| Capital | Profit |
| Gearing | Funding |
| Dividends/Distribution | Treasury |
| Key Executives | Forex/Derivatives/Balance |
| Management Quality | Sheet Management |
| Research & Development | |

## Non-entrepreneurial

**Strategic**

**Operational**

Crisis Management
Political/Regulatory Change
Infrastructure/Organisation
Quality
Pollution/Environment
Suppliers
HR Strategy
Staff Quality
Personal Development
Technology
IT Strategy
PR/Corporate Affairs

Legal/Regulatory Compliance
Credit/Counterparty
Stock/Receivables
Business Processes
Systems
Fire/Explosion/Adverse Weather
Tax/VAT
Accounting
Equipment
Physical Security/Entry
HR Policy
Employee Practices
Training
Health & Safety
Industrial Accidents

Decisions on the above can be assessed for the effect of risks and possible consequences on: investors and stakeholder perceptions; cash flow; quality and customer service; brand and image; share price; profits and profitability; survival; generation of long-term value; PR and corporate relations.

➤        ➤        ➤

# 7

# Strategic Planning, Choice and the Risk Factor

The continuous cycle of improvement in the management of business processes was introduced earlier. Each of the processes follows a logical sequence where the next is not considered until the previous has been concluded. The whole cycle is then reconsidered before the strategic planning process is concluded. Many organisations may see strategic planning as an annual exercise. Our belief and assumption used here, is that strategic planning is an ongoing, at least monthly and maybe weekly management process. Each time the opportunities for improvement are reviewed, they may lead to revised or new strategic direction.

The five elements are (**DRIMI**):

➤ **Direction** (what do we want to do?).

➤ **Resources** (what do we need to do it?).

➤ **Implementation** (how, i.e. through what processes, are we going to do it?).

➤ How are we going to **Measure** how we are performing?

➤ When we review how we are doing, where can we see ways to **Improve**?

Direction is all about the strategic direction in which we wish to take the business, including a consideration of previous direction.

Resources is all about the various different resources we have at our disposal and that we might otherwise need in order to deliver a chosen direction. These would typically include: people, capital assets, production facilities, distribution networks, information systems capability, finance, brand, intellectual property and other intangible assets, etc.

Implementation is about the management and business processes through which we will achieve our chosen direction. It is also about the systems that support such processes. (Note: many organisations in the past have selected or acquired systems before making the processes fit them. We believe the reverse is the correct order. Design or redesign the processes and then modify or acquire assistance to support the delivery).

Measurement and control is about how we assess our performance against predetermined objectives and what control processes are necessary to ensure that delivery.

Improvement is about recognising and understanding the opportunities to learn and grow when we review our progress against the agreed direction. There is a simple three-question format to this review process that is transportable to all such reviews or appraisals in any circumstances across the organisation. (Incidentally, they are highly appropriate in personal life as well):

> ➤    What has gone well since we last met?
> ➤    Where are the opportunities to improve?
> ➤    Overall how well have we done?

It is worthwhile considering how all of the five stages inform and revise our view of strategic direction. In all of these phases of the management processes, what questions need to be asked about alternatives, risks, consequences and eventual choices? Once again, it starts with strategy.

### A Practical Example

So, some of you may be saying "I haven't got time for all this detail". So how much time have you got to plan your success or even your survival in highly competitive and complex markets, including a consideration of how to make risk work?

Here is a practical example. Many years ago, we were asked to help one of the largest NHS Trusts in the UK recover from serious financial problems. It quickly became clear that the three major difficulties were:

> ➤ inadequacy of financial controls;
> ➤ a total absence of strategic planning; and
> ➤ inefficient, time-consuming management practices.

The first was resolved by eliminating the back-pocket accounting and introducing rigorous, budgetary control. The second by designing and implementing strategic planning processes similar to those recommended in this book (as well as the processes for management of risk which saved the organisation £250,000 a year). The third was resolved by introducing carefully designed management processes.

At first, the Chief Executive was reluctant to go ahead with the management process exercise. "My diary is already completely full without adding more meetings" he said. We promised him that the result of introducing this approach would release large chunks of time. We set about redesigning the top eight management processes by which the whole organisation would be run, starting with the strategic planning process. Each process was summarised on one sheet of paper. Having been accepted, within three months the organisation was running twice as efficiently as it had ever done and the Chief Executive was delighted.

There are two points to this chapter. The first is that every organisation (as indeed every individual) has choices in everything that they do. The second is that by introducing carefully designed and crafted management and business processes which closely fit the organisation and its culture and, starting with strategic planning and running through the entire improvement cycle help to ensure efficiency, add growth and new directions at every stage.

We have worked with organisations introducing this approach over and over. Indeed, we have even introduced them into our own lives and businesses. The initial effort and the integration into the organisation's daily management processes will pay growing dividends indefinitely. The only other thing that we would add is the importance of risk being a constructive and objective consideration at every stage of the management process cycle.

➤     ➤     ➤

# 8

# Assessing the Risk Factor in Strategic Choices

The Risk Factor is that quantifiable or unquantifiable element in the business or organisation which, when recognised and managed can produce enhanced profits, gains or other positive benefits or minimise loss or damage to the value or sustainability of the business.

## Informing Strategic Choices

As the continuous cycle of improvement shows earlier, eventually strategic planning evolves into the management of operations. We have choices in everything that we do and isn't it better when they are informed by considerations such as the strategic context and the potential impact of risk?

When considering operational risk, it is useful to classify by time and cause, likelihood and impact. This approach is also transportable to project management. A standard approach would be to ask the key personnel and a random selection of others "what are the top six risks to delivery as you see them?" The respondents would also propose a value between one and ten for their likely probability and the impact of each risk if it was to eventualise (with ten being the most likely or greatest impact and one being the least).

In reviewing the proposed or revised operations, it is desirable to look at a number of considerations in each stage of the process. These could include:

➤ What is the purpose of this process;
➤ What is the nature of the risks involved;
➤ What are the resources required;
➤ What is the scale of the risk;
➤ What are the potential benefits;
➤ What are the mitigating factors;
➤ What contingency or contingencies do we have in place or planned;
➤ What limitations are there to our desired course of action.

There will need to be processes for collecting information, agreed methods of analysis, the creation of a risk database. It is inevitable that this will involve some degree of complexity and organisation. It is also important to be absolutely clear about responsibility and accountability.

### Financial Sector Case Study

In 1985, we were brought in to introduce treasury management into a major financial institution. They previously had no real understanding of what this involved and consequently had neither the skills nor processes and systems to plan for, and avoid, the inevitable risks and capture the opportunities which arose therefrom.

Now this might seem somewhat surprising considering the organisation had many billions of pounds under management. Not only was it not unusual in its sector however, but also they later became the first institution of their type in the UK to introduce risk management.

Using the processes described above, during the next six months we created a treasury function as sophisticated as any in that sector. Shortly afterwards the possibility developed of using derivatives and other financial management techniques not only to manage the balance sheet but also to facilitate the creation of a sophisticated range of new financial products.

Unfortunately, the sector regulator had serious misgivings about the responsibility and accountability of such organisations for using the sophisticated tools and was somewhat reluctant to grant permission to any organisation. It looked like it would be many years before permission was forthcoming. However, we rigorously applied a similar set of processes, as well as understanding the needs and wishes of the regulator and best practice in the banking community.

Our challenge to the regulator was "please do not refuse us permission without a hearing. Set us the tests, standards and barriers that we have to overcome and we shall meet those, using the auditors to assess and confirm our readiness before we come back to you." This approach was highly successful. They became the first such institution to be granted these wider financial powers while several of their larger competitors took two years or more to achieve the same standard. As a consequence they became, and remained, highly competitive in a sector with benefits to brand, customer service and profitability.

## Making Informed Choices

Understanding and managing corporate risk is fundamental to making informed choices in the context of strategic management. Understanding of risk is also fundamental to a differentiated strategy. What are the choices available to us? What are the potential rewards? What are the potential risks? Informed choices lead to objective processes, facilitating implementation, evolution and revision of the strategy.

During the preparation of this book we spent some time trying to compose a useful mnemonic for everyday use in the consideration of risk in any business decision. Whimsical though it may be, we came up with CROPPERS, which stands for:

> What are the **Choices**?
> What are the **Risks**?
> What are the **Opportunities**?
> What are the **Probabilities** of these opportunities and risks?
> What are the **Processes** needed to effect the choices?
> **Evaluate** all the alternatives.
> Assess the **Return**, as overall value added in qualitative and quantitative terms.
> **Select** the optimum way forward.

This succinctly captures a set of thought processes that is reusable in a multitude of different business and organisational situations requiring a decision.

# 9

# The Risk Factor in Investment and Development Decisions

There have been many excellent textbooks on the subject of capital investment. Much theory has also been written about the mathematics of capital investment decisions. At university in 1967, Modigliani & Miller's theory was very much in fashion. It has remained as one of the models of capital investment decisions ever since. The only regret was that, while theoretically sound, in practice it would not have the slightest relevance for a business manager.

Modelling of management decisions is a science in itself. From decision-based theory to capital investment models, there is some validity in attempting to capture the mathematics of seemingly rational choice.

From 1974 working as an information systems consultant, one role was to review the effectiveness of new systems implementations. One of the clients had purchased a new computer. We asked them the basis for their business decision. They had many similar systems to choose from. "In the end, we decided to buy from the last computer salesman who came through the door" said the Managing Director. So much for science.

The advent of business process management has moved things forward for many organisations. While intuition and enterprise are increasingly valuable commodities in fast changing competitive markets, there is still a place for complementary structured rational thinking.

In the case of investment decisions there are three different main priorities:

➤ 'Business as Usual';
➤ Business Development;
➤ Business Investment.

### Business as Usual

This involves the regular, especially capital, investment decisions required to sustain business continuity as it is at the present. So, for example, from time to time information systems need to be renewed or updated; machines need to be replaced; new premises are required, etc.

### Business Development

This refers to the investment required to grow the existing business without changing its overall nature or that of a significant part of it.

### Business Investment

This is the type of investment that relates to acquiring new businesses and/or creating a new business entity or segment within the existing business structure.

Apart from the obvious distinctions, the value of this differentiation is in the order of priorities. Capital assets and related resources are a finite commodity. The presumption therefore is that the scarce resources will be invested in the priority order as listed above. In other words, in theory, no investment would be made in business development or new businesses if there is insufficient capital to go beyond business as usual.

This overlooks two very important considerations however. The first one is, what are the risks inherent in the decisions themselves and the overall priorities? The second involves three key aspects of investment decisions related to business as usual: what are we currently doing that we no longer need to do and still deliver the strategic plan; what could we change or do differently and still achieve the same ends; and what capital resources will be released by implementing these decisions which can be made available for business development and business investment?

We still find it extraordinary that in the consideration of the various strategic options in the planning process, even some of the most sophisticated businesses still do not ask themselves the question, "what do we no longer need to do or could we do differently to achieve the same strategic aims"?

## The Basis of Capital Investment Decisions

All capital investment decisions involve risk. One of the reasons why is because there is usually a range of alternatives, with the different ways to achieve the strategic goals all competing for the same capital resources. Going back to the risk considerations mentioned earlier, we would want to review which decisions, in delivering the strategic objectives, maximise the profit, gains or benefits, sustain or enhance long-term value at the same time ensuring that potential losses or damage to the brand or corporate value are minimised. In other words what are the key Risk Factors in these capital investment decisions and what is the potential impact?

Of course cost of capital is a key consideration, but (apart from whether the organisation can afford that cost) it is just as important to consider the tangible and intangible gains and the other tangible or intangible costs or potential risk consequences.

The best capital investment management theory and practice encourages consideration of risk at every stage of the investment decision process. In practise, we see a consideration of the Risk Factors as being inextricable from the investment evaluation. The overall analysis will include reviewing all the opportunities and positives, which may flow therefrom in conjunction with all the alternatives and the potential risks or consequences of each of these. The risk/reward equation involves a three-dimensional consideration of: profits, gains or benefits; negative consequences of other alternative courses avoided; opportunity costs of not pursuing a particular choice; and potential loss or damage arising from this or other choices.

What we like about risk-adjusted rate-of-return and portfolio-theory is the mathematical estimation of Risk Factors. In practice, however, too much science could be counterproductive. That is not to say that we don't advocate a balance between science and art in investment decisions, that we do recommend simplicity (and the template approach in the appendix is just one example in relation to the overall management of risk).

For example, applying the 'top six risks' approach to investment decisions is an excellent way to augment their financial analysis in deciding the way forward between a number of different competing alternatives. The consideration of alternatives goes well beyond their investment choices. It also relates to the alternative uses of the finance and resources in the existing business, including pluses and minuses of doing nothing at all.

Especially with the advent of globalisation and the power of the Internet, the economy in general and markets in particular are moving so fast that capital investment decisions may not be able to be made with the same time for reflection as might have existed in the past. There has always been value in considering the Risk Factors and these have become even more important as the criticality of making the right decision has increased further.

As with all the strategic and operational decisions, at the end of the day it comes back to questions, questions and more questions. We want to encourage objectively enquiring organisations with individuals empowered to contribute and be involved in many decisions that they may have been excluded from in the past. The best organisations now recognise that everyone can make a potential conclusion, not only because anyone can have a good idea but also because corporate and organisational success is now fundamentally based on their ownership by the whole organisation of strategic decisions and their practical implementation.

People are now unquestionably recognised as the key capital resource. Escalating transfer fees for footballers demonstrated that point decades ago. In other words, people are also the key Risk Factor.

➤    ➤    ➤

# PART C

# Implementing
# the Risk Factor

# 10

# Risk Strategy

We have now reached the core of this book, which relates to the eight key elements involved in implementing the Risk Factor approach into the organisation's management and business processes. We begin by reviewing the risk strategy (which is inseparable from and integrated into the overall business strategy) before moving to the seven elements related to the implementation of that strategy.

The pattern in this section of the book and especially in the appendices is set. It now becomes a matter of questions, questions and more questions. So let us begin:

- Do you have a comprehensive strategy for handling risk?
- Is this strategy committed to paper?
- Is this strategy integrated within the organisation's corporate strategy?
- Has the organisation clearly defined what it means by a strategy?
- How have you defined risk?
- Does the strategy embrace all risks?
- What risks have you excluded and if so, for what specific reasons?
- How are priorities attached and integrated to other business decisions?
- What do we (you) mean by a strategy for managing risk?

The key factors in the risk strategy are that:

> ➤ It should be planned thoroughly;
> ➤ It should be integrated into the overall strategy;
> ➤ There must be clearly defined links to the decision making process.

Risk strategy sits at the strategic level of the management process and will benefit from incorporation within the organisation's overall strategic planning and budgeting activity.

An important point here is the creation of a strategy that actually reflects your organisation. Too often a strategy is 'borrowed' from another organisation, knowingly or otherwise and altered or amended to fit the host organisation. This misses one of the key benefits or elements of the overall process, which is the hard slog of learning what 'it' is all about for your business. This works best as an intuitive, iterative process.

This process of compiling your own corporate or risk strategy can of course benefit from following a sound template, particularly if this reflects your line of business, trade, speciality or discipline. This enquiry based template approach is adopted throughout most of the rest of the book.

From this recommended development process will emerge an initial view of the extent of the overall task that the organisation is embarking on. It should provide an indication of the necessary action to further develop the draft strategy.

It is also important to establish at the earliest point a process for continual refinement and improvement, reflecting feedback from a wide variety or spectrum of views. Moreover time set aside and objectives to be achieved from the process will need to be reflected in the overall management processes.

The nomination of one person with ultimate responsibility and accountability, and the authority and support of the Board of directors to champion the role throughout the organisation, is going to be absolutely essential if the organisation is to succeed. This does not imply that we recommend the setting up of a function to manage risk. If this is the preferred route to the organisation, it should ideally be a temporary arrangement by way of 'kick starting' the organisation's efforts until the processes can be integrated into the organisation's daily *modus operandi.*

## A Rigorous Approach to Risk Strategy

The successful management of risk requires a rigorous approach that begins with a coherent strategy. This, whilst incorporating the organisation's business objectives also states the organisation's approach within the following key headings. It establishes the procedures for systematising the process of the handling of risk.

The strategy should embrace and incorporate the following seven key headings, each prepared and presented in a consistent, supportive and standardised way:

- Risk (Action) Planning
- Risk Information Flow
- Risk Education (&Training)
- Risk Process Structure
- Risk Recording
- Risk Handling
- Risk Assurance (Audit & Compliance)

The success of the entire corporate approach to the management of risk depends on the organisation's ability to commit to paper in clear, concise and unequivocal terms, the language and definition that will be utilised throughout. In addition, it is recommended that you incorporate a mechanism for the ongoing recognition of all the risks that an organisation faces.

The risk study should:

- Recognise the role of people and machines;
- Standardise and allow for the identification of risk;
- Evaluate potential risks considering the impact and likelihood.

In addition, strategies for risk should be updated in the event of significant changes in the organisation's strategic planning and/or circumstances.

More and more, corporate management is being characterised as project management. Whether or not this is the case in your organisation it is important for there to be links between the management of risk and project management.

Project management has been described as a discipline for 'doers', the people who turn dreams into reality and business strategy into success. (Jim Reynolds Products & Services Director – Mercury Communications Ltd, in the preface to Robert Buttrick's book 'The Project Workout") (FT Pitman Publishing ISBN 0-273-62680-9).

It is inevitable that the management of risk will be integrated into forward planning. It is also desirable that energy will be devoted to reporting risk rather than failure, loss or damage. This will be clear evidence that the proactive approach we recommend is working as planned.

## Integrating the Risk Strategy

The risk strategy should be managed and implemented from the top of the organisation, starting with the Chief Executive or Managing Director all the way down and through every level. Risk awareness should become second nature for everyone. An openness of culture will also encourage understanding and feedback about the Risk Factors in practice.

Risk should be integrated seamlessly into the overall strategy - clearly defined, communicated and understood by everyone. Ownership and accountability are just as fundamental in risk awareness and the management of risk as in the overall management processes in the modern business organisation. The reasoning is very simple. It relates to the intentionally positive or negative impacts of risk on the creation of stakeholder values.

We are not talking here about taking more or greater risks, rather we are looking for a better understanding of risk and a culture that makes risk work for you.

Most modern businesses and organisations cannot afford to operate in a ponderous way. For many years, in the US and Japan, we have seen companies sustaining a far higher price to earnings ratio than in Europe. Such companies have existed in an economic environment where it was much easier to start up, operate, flex and adapt. Now, with the advent of globalisation and the Internet the new order of enterprise throughout the world has to create and sustain much more effective income generation on the same asset base.

Managing risk therefore becomes more a matter of understanding and seizing the opportunity or challenge, thereby maximising value creation and/or minimising potential loss of value, rather than structure and control. The productive assets are now mainly people, customers, employees and partners and therefore opportunistically all circumstantial. So they are the key Risk Factor.

Technology and the globalisation of markets have combined to transform the world economy. Value generation capability and therefore market value of the old economy stocks has become relatively more inhibited. Although there may be a higher rate of, and more spectacular failure in, the new economy, as companies and investors adjust to the greater dynamism and volatility, those that are able to continuously improve and reinvent themselves will thrive, thereby rewriting the old order.

As mentioned elsewhere, it brings new and growing challenges to regulation. The deregulation of the old utilities and financial markets has become an inevitable part of a move towards greater freedom and self-regulation. While stock markets, the accounting profession, banking and other major sectors will continue to rationalise on a global scale, pragmatically, the authorities will begin to realise the consequences for regulation.

Globalisation takes entrepreneurial practise beyond all geographical boundaries. The pace and incentive for invention and value creation will always exceed the ability of the authorities to keep up. It should be recognised, however, that for many, if not most, organisations the growing freedoms will represent both a threat as well as an opportunity unless the Risk Factors are regularly reviewed and well understood.

Volatility will continue to increase. As investment funds not only grow but also become pan-global, especially tracker funds will have to invest in increasingly risky stocks or be left with sub-optimal performance. The prices of the high-flying stocks may be exaggerated by scarcity value. The stretch between the best and worst performers, high cap and low cap stocks will increase. Eventually, the old economy companies will either have to reinvent themselves or wind up, pay back the capital and go home.

Raising capital could become problematic for many companies. This is not to say that there will not be capital available. However, small and medium cap companies, undervalued by the market may not wish to raise capital at those prices. With the high-flying mega corporations, however, cash flow management may become a perennial problem except for the very best.

In the meantime, corporations will have to balance creation of long-term shareholder value, managing short-term expectations and awareness and response to wider stakeholder priorities.

The above is a summary of some of the main macro Risk Factors. Most companies whether large or small will feel some or even a substantial, direct or indirect impact. We say again, as with corporate strategy, risk strategy and implementation should become part of the daily routine. Openness of objectives, information, understanding and feedback will be fundamental so that the wider organisation takes account of the Risk Factors in a proactive, empowered way. Synergy and devolved accountability will be desirable so that the organisation can react and adapt as appropriate.

## Corporate Goals and Implementation

Corporate goals should be widely shared and owned, responsive to the marketplace, stakeholders and the organisation. Nothing less than the best will do. Those organisations that are not prepared to engage with, or in, the new economy may either have to carve their own niche or accept regressive or under performance.

Part of the Risk Factor approach is to continually ask the questions:

> ➤ What did we set out to do?
> ➤ What are we actually doing?
> ➤ What if anything do we need to take account of or change?
> ➤ What are the consequences of continuing to do what we set out to do?
> ➤ What are the consequences of change?

Thought processes such as these will enable the organisation to make decisions, flex and adapt with an objective and up-to-date understanding of their circumstances, the opportunities, a proactive view of the risks and the relative consequences of a chosen route.

Clearly defined goals and objectives should be complemented by a broad and thorough understanding of the Risk Factors, and a qualitative and quantitative assessment of the potential consequences on different courses of action. The chosen route will have taken account of all these factors, with a conscious awareness and understanding of risk supported by an organisation that is able and willing to flex and adapt where appropriate.

# 11

# Risk (Action) Planning

Our intention is not in any sense to be prescriptive. Rather it is to create a climate of constructive inquiry and understanding. The approach is essentially positive, seeking to capitalise on the optimum opportunity, best strategic analysis and awareness of the Risk Factors and create, while minimising potentially adverse circumstances. These would include not just losses but also opportunity cost and missed benefits.

Later we shall come to the specifics of handling risk. Having identified and set out the overall corporate strategy together with the specific risk strategy, the next step is planning the actions to take. Some may involve clearly understood strategic steps, optimising the overall value creation in the context of the known risks. Others will imply taking specific steps to capitalise on the Risk Factors, at the very least to manage or minimise their potential consequences.

The questions here include:

➤ Is there a plan for effectively handling risk?

➤ Is this planning clearly documented?

➤ Is the plan integrated within the organisation's overall planning activity?

➤ Is this plan regularly updated to reflect lessons learnt and potential improvements?

➤ Does the plan include straightforward targets, objectives and deadlines?

### Risk Planning in Action

The overall purpose is to effectively manage implementation of the strategy including those parts identified to take account of risk. There will be a clearly identified programme of activities in keeping with the strategy and related to the management processes, especially the organisation's decision-making process.

This part of the risk process is not in addition to the main processes but should improve what the organisation already does. All business activities involve risk. Consequently, every manager in the organisation should have similar understanding, taking the same hard and focussed approach to managing risks. It is an integral part of every day management activity at all levels.

The previous chapter was set at the strategic and policy level. The present element relates to the many tactical levels of the organisation.

## *What are the Benefits of Managing Risk?*

Ask yourself why this remains an issue? Maybe the difficulty is interpreting the theory and applying it in a practical situation. Whatever the reason, look around your actual market place or sector. Talk to the other people whose organisations you respect as leaders. The next time you meet a management consultant or business adviser ask them what is happening with the managing risk function. Arthur Andersen, respected world-wide for their thorough approach to consultancy published a best practice guide called 'Positive Risk Management".

A story from a real life skiing incident that happened to Mark Webb is another interesting analogy and demonstrates the 'domino effect" which is so often entwined with risk.

Waiting for an automated ski lift, he took a glove off briefly, failing to notice that he had dropped a ski stick. Due to the crush of skiers, it was a few seconds before he missed the stick, now well behind him. A fellow skier picked it up and Mark, now close to the lift access gates, leant back to retrieve the pole. In doing so his skis became unweighted causing him to slide off at speed, limboing under the safety gate at the moment the ski lift arrived to collect the next rank of skiers from the platform.

Mark received a bang to the shoulder as he was caught up by the footrest and spun into the metal protective fencing. All this was before the attendant was aware of what was happening and able to hit the emergency button, preventing further damage or injury.

The point to the story is that in corporate life as well as in personal life, an event causing injury, damage or loss can come about as a result of a series of smaller often insignificant yet inter-linked events, each of which on its own seems innocuous. Hence the reference to what is known as the domino theory.

We live in the Knowledge Era. The speed of response to information and the sharing and understanding of accurate knowledge is a business differentiator. There is potentially real competitive advantage in implementing a systematic and organised attempt to use knowledge to improve performance. Applying the combined power of computer technology and the Internet, together with best practice in your sector or industry is the way to keep pace with developments.

We are also in the era of what has been labelled the digital nervous system (DNS), which is also because of ever increasing competitiveness. As the pace of change accelerates so survival often depends on the speed at which organisations can respond to changes in their environment. This is one of the reasons why we used the analogy between the human and corporate body/mind.

Everywhere traditional business models are being turned on their head. Barriers to entry are falling and competition is intensifying There is no substitute for being prepared to effectively handle both the expected and the unexpected.

### What do we Mean by Managing Risk?

The words 'managing' and 'risk' are increasingly being connected and associated with an ever expanding variety of task specific services and products, progressively leading to the creation of a plethora of meanings and associations.

This has lead to an overuse (and maybe even abuse) of the words and their meanings. This may have created much confusion and a lack of clarity and understanding amongst many within the business community.

It can perhaps even be argued that the over exposure to these particular words has created a sense of lethargy towards the subject. This is despite the efforts of many well-intended individuals. These attitudes may have contributed to a relative failure of this core management skill to gain the acceptance, recognition and attention at a senior level within organisations that it merits and needs.

This could be said to be an advantage for those organisations that are already ahead of the game. The management of risk is increasingly becoming a core discipline, by choice rather than imposition.

Being in business or public service means taking decisions, all of which involve risk. The only question is one of the extent of risk acceptance. If you were to provide for every eventuality, the organisation would soon be paralysed.

One aim should be to know as many of the risks to which your business is exposed. On the other hand life is full of those 'little' surprises, which appear from nowhere to test managers (even when they are on a skiing holiday!) Therefore what also matters is how you handle this risk (event) as and when it occurs. Maybe what is even more important is the processes you have in place to understand the risk and how it occurred and what you can learn which will be of benefit for the organisation in the future. The Japanese are well known for their business successes, which is often connected with quality matters. This has often been associated with CANI – continuous and never-ending improvement.

Our version for business success through managing risk is PANI – progressive and never-ending improvement, which many clients see as a PAIN when first introducing the concepts being explored in this publication.

### Outdated Views of Managing Risk

Responding to a questionnaire on the subject matter, a significant number of participants made these and similar observations:

➤ "Risk Management? - That's what the Insurance Department does".

➤ "Risk Management? - Our Risk Manager does that."

➤ "Risk Management is boring, it's nothing to do with me."

➤ "Risk Management - I don't want to do it."

➤ "Risk Management has had its day"

➤ "Risk Management? We don't need it, we already have a Health & Safety Department"

➤          ➤          ➤

# 12

# Risk Information Flow

Objective management of risk is part of a continuous cycle of understanding, learning, improving and informing the strategic direction. The process for identifying, understanding and managing risks and opportunities should be common and consistent across the whole organisation.

The risk information system should be a mechanism for Risk Factors, which allows all adverse events, consequences and significant control weaknesses to be communicated to every appropriate manager, executive or director.

Clearly in this book, we are describing a proactive strategy and process for managing risk. Even now, for many organisations the first step may be to put in place a formal process for identifying and managing risk. All the best organisations that we work with, are able to rapidly move to the next stage where managing with an awareness of the Risk Factors has become second nature, integrated into the strategic and implementation management processes.

Management and business processes only work well when supported by excellent, flexible and adaptable information systems. Ideally, these will be based on a sound and up-to-date technology platform; supported by state-of-the-art responsive software. The ability to drill down, compare and integrate information across and outside the organisation on a real-time basis is fundamental to staying ahead of the game.

Information systems do not always provide the right information at the right time, especially in new or unexpected circumstances. We still continue to be stunned by the apparent inflexibility of some organisations to produce information on the needs must basis as opposed to sitting paralysed if the IT systems cannot cope.

In the rapidly changing 21st century a seat of the pants, 80:20 approach may be increasingly necessary. There is seemingly limitless information available on the World Wide Web which, together with sophisticated modelling tools and techniques, creativity and lateral thinking can produce sufficient understanding to make an informed decision especially where differentiating between alternatives. It is no surprise that creative, lateral thinkers (or 'plants' in the Belbin scheme of things) are increasingly being sought through psychometric testing by leading-edge organisations.

We have become used to structured management information and reporting processes. It is inflexibility of such timetables and the lack of evolution of management reports that has often for all practical purposes made such reporting all but redundant. While it may be necessary to explain past actions, when the regulator calls or the market has been surprised by under-performance, the ability to explain past actions is becoming far less important than the capability of planning for or predicting the future.

Only seven or eight years ago, Terry was working with a public sector organisation whose monthly reporting timetable to the regulators was 20 calendar days. This was something of a shock compared with previous corporate sector experience of producing a trial balance for the annual accounts within three days.

The regulator proposed a reduction to fifteen days. Some organisations could not even report within a calendar month, which for them made the whole process farcical. The team was asked to do a feasibility study for producing information within five days. They came back 48 hours later to say that this was not possible. However, they had managed to achieve a timetable of eight days!

When this was implemented they rapidly found not only that they were accorded more leeway and freedom by their regulator, but also they were first allowed two and later three-monthly reporting due to the revised belief in the quality of management processes.

For most organisations, the implicit regulator is the marketplace itself. With a reactive, structured and controlled approach to the management of risk, together with an incomplete awareness and understanding of the Risk Factors the consequence is likely to be that the organisation is a market follower, rather than leader.

Information flows in general, but especially those related to risk awareness and understanding, need to be top down, bottom up, lateral, diagonal and matrix, structuring and restructuring so as to be responsive to market and organisation dynamics.

# Key Risk Information

Some of the key questions here are:

> What are the risks facing your organisation?
> What are the priorities?
> What is risk costing your organisation?
> Is the information computerised to aid interpretation?
> Is it capable of adapting and flexing rapidly to new circumstances?

Information is crucial to the promotion of any activity involving specific attention on risk issues. The flow of information needs and requires conscious thought, logical design, deliberate action and must be fit for the organisation.

What do we mean by the flow of information? We mean relevant individuals having ready and rapid access to the risk information necessary to make timely and appropriate decisions. Without this, true empowerment could be progressively undermined.

How else will any person within the organisation know what is expected of them?

Take for a moment the analogy of how the finance department works. Financial information is collected, stored, analysed, used and interpreted. Finance as a function has had to become progressively more responsive. Whilst in both the corporate and public sectors there may still exist substantial pockets of old practices, leading edge management now needs and demands as up-to-date and relevant information as possible, in order to make high quality decisions.

As a parallel, there has been a gradual drift away from historical accounting information towards management accounting information, modelling, simulation and scenario planning. In the very best organisations, decision-makers are not only numerate but also instinctive and intuitive in collating and using quantitative and qualitative measures. By the time the monthly report emerges, they can not only explain the reasons for their departures from expected performance, but how they have already implemented the necessary changes and can predict the positive consequences for the following period.

The same aspirations and standards are applicable to optimising strategic outcomes taking account of all the known and relevant Risk Factors.

There are benefits in presenting and considering information in 'standard' forms and standard 'units of currency'. This enables objective comparison, together with presentation in a style that is understood by not only those within the organisation but also those external to the business and even in different countries and cultures. Even the very best quality information, is of little use however if it is either not relevant or not easily understood. Garbage has no value no matter how fast it is produced.

It goes without saying that unreliable, inconsistent or apparently conflicting information can either undermine the quality decisions or lead to differential or under performance.

During the strategic planning process, information can be collected, collated and reviewed at a slightly more leisurely pace. The implementation processes however require rapid, responsive, reactive and relevant information, especially in respect of anticipated Risk Factors or unexpected events and consequences.

The flow of (risk) information should be designed with the (risk) assurance procedure in sharp focus. This will greatly assist with the process of each planning and managing activity promoting easier and more effective auditing.

Risk information and assurance is no longer restricted to the audit process. It needs to be interactive with the daily management processes. Internal audit has evolved to provide and support this function and that is all well and good. This is the ideal. The involvement of audit personnel will also minimise the tendency for 're-inventing the wheel'; thereby reducing the chance for gaps in the system of checks.

➢    ➢    ➢

# 13

# Risk Education (& Training)

Consider for a moment the difference between a risk manager and a manager of risk. Leaving aside the financial management of risk, the discipline is still in its relative infancy. Fifteen years ago there were few if any textbooks on the management of risk, which weren't in effect insurance manuals. With the emergence of Risk Magazine, The Treasurer and other similar organs, the subject has been brought into greater prominence. Even now, however, the bent is very much towards financial risk and governance.

So what is the difference between a risk manager and a manager of risk? A risk manager is someone practised or skilled in the profession of managing risk. A manager of risk is someone who carries out day-to-day leadership or managerial responsibilities with an awareness of risk and how to make it work for you.

Even now, the teaching of the management of risk in business schools is largely absorbed within other disciplines and although some universities do offer courses in Risk Management, many professionals, trainers, consultants, etc. can teach the principles of corporate governance. The authors themselves would be regarded as trainers of managing risk and risk handling. The approach, however, and indeed the best way forward is to facilitate awareness and experiential understanding. Especially when managing risk, it is better to have an army of thinkers and implementers rather than slavish doers.

In an ideal world all of management would be trained to be aware of and factor risk into every-day decisions. Leading by example, facilitating understanding and seizing on every departure from plan as a learning opportunity, they would then become 'tour guides' in the management of risk for everyone in the organisation.

We need to start somewhere, however. To create a risk-aware and optimising culture, you need some structure and organisation to get the ball rolling. Again risk has traditionally been seen as having negative connotations. A key part of the creation of a successful risk-aware culture is to encourage a climate of opportunity and positivity.

### Key Questions for Risk Education and Training

➤ Do you have a specific budget allocated to risk training?
➤ Do you have records of risk training within the organisation?
➤ Do all employees clearly understand the organisation's risk strategy?
➤ Are all employees made aware of the organisation's risk policy?
➤ Do you allocate a specific budget for risk handling issues?

### What does Risk Education and Training Include?

As always it starts with communication. The organisation needs to demonstrate their commitment to the management of risk and this starts with the Chief Executive and the top team. The management of risk should no longer be kept in a box and treated as a mystical, technical discipline somewhat separated from the everyday affairs.

A number of different specific exercises have in the past worked well to stimulate the debate and understanding and create the momentum for the organisation of risk awareness.

For example, a risk brain-storming session by the top team. It could be based around the organisation's core operations, as starting with strategy and flowing through to implementation. Alternatively, it works extremely well where the organisation is in the throes of or contemplating a major capital project or business development. Whatever is chosen, a key advantage is in having a central focus to introduce the topic of risk and risk awareness.

Another exercise that has worked very well is to bring together the wider team (in one case this involved 60 or 70 managers) again with a central focus as above. Commencing with presentations by the key directors or executives on the strategy and implementation, it can then break out into smaller 'study groups', each of which brain-storms what they thought to be the main areas of risk.

The outputs are then collected, sifted and grouped together into main headings such as e.g. the core disciplines of the organisation (strategic, marketing, sales, manufacture, finance, HR, IT, etc.). Those present can be regrouped with a mix of disciplines in each to consider one of the identified areas per group. The purpose being to highlight the core risks, estimate the probability and impact and suggest ways of moving forward.

Each group then presents to the overall assembly for wider understanding. All the outputs are collected together and distributed later to those who have attended. It may be helpful to have independent observers of the process to make appropriate helpful observations. They can also ensure a clean process, especially helping to avoid domination by the top team. Informal discussions with all the participants is a way to ensure that all the real issues are teased out.

It is important to stress that these are but two examples of how to stimulate a natural and spontaneous awareness and understanding of risk in your organisation. At the end of the day it is most important that the training, education and awareness processes should fit easily into the culture. That is not to say, that many managers and staff will not find risk something of a new discipline, investing it with many of their own expectations and where relevant past experience. The key is to facilitate the process whereby management with awareness of risks becomes second nature.

# Education and Training

What is the difference? Remember your own experiences in school or college where you were taught perhaps by the teacher standing at the front of the class using chalk to mark the blackboard and for you to copy down the words of wisdom. How well did that approach work for you?

Later techniques utilised televisions, videos and even role-plays. On the other hand, how much better did training work when you were able to find your own way to the knowledge and understanding through participation, learning in a safe environment, being able to experiment – this process is known as 'Simulation Training'. Very often the difference is being in the right culture, facilitated by a trainer that knows and understands and has the skills necessary to create the best opportunity for learning.

Simulation training can be a most appropriate method for introducing and continuing the task of managing risk in an organisation. At the outset it is important that everyone involved knows what their role is (especially in the event of a disaster). Whatever else the organisation does, the process starts and ends with communication. The only worthwhile purpose of communication is awareness and understanding, otherwise you are wasting your time and money. The question is "is the message being received and understood, and how do you know".

Simulation training also enables the process of risk handling and its management to be integrated throughout an organisation by actually delivering business risk education to all levels. Being fun and specific to a client's business at the same time it emulates the best parts of an individual's learning process and promotes rapid understanding of the corporate risk message.

So what might you anticipate when you first introduce the topic of risk? We have already considered earlier, some of the conditioned responses. The point is whatever topic to introduce there may always be some people and managers who think it is nothing to do with them and is somebody else's responsibility. So the skill is in creating interest and a vested reason to learn.

We are not talking about building an understanding of risk into the reward or motivation package. In an ideal world you will already have an enterprising or empowering culture. With a mix of qualitative and quantitative goals shared and owned across the organisation, what you then need to do is to build in the positive challenge and opportunity arising from managing with an objective understanding of risk. At the very least, without inhibiting the organisation's momentum, every single manager needs an awareness of risk, its potential impact on the organisation, and an understanding of the specific risks in their own area of responsibility.

Whatever process is used to promote an awareness and understanding of risk and to introduce the management of risk into the mainstream management and business processes, communication will be central. As many organisations have found, the best way to ensure a successful communication and understanding of information is to test the process. In very large organisations, communications audit and the use of focus groups has been very successful. In small organisations there is no substitute for 'management by walking around' (MBWA), having informal conversations to get a feel for people's broad understanding.

In other words, whatever the processes used to get risk into the organisation, test them to make sure that they're working on an ongoing basis and that feedback received from individuals is not only acknowledged but acted upon whenever practical.

Since the advent of corporate governance, many organisations have introduced the management of risk and control procedures as a rigid discipline. We do not suggest that this will not work, however our own experience suggests that it is the methods, which achieve broad ownership and understanding, which will lead to instinctive and objective management of risk which minimises potential threats whilst at the same time maximising opportunity.

## *Introducing the Skills of Managing Risk*

Remember we are talking here of identifying, understanding and managing with an awareness of the Risk Factors. What are the factors that can be made to work for you? What are those that you need to take account of? What are the factors that could lead to loss of or damage to value or benefits and those which can be turned to advantage to create sustainable value at a managed level of risk?

So what are the skills of a manager of risk? In many respects they are the same as those of a skilful manager. We are not talking about traditional values here, but rather those that will thrive in the global, high technology markets of the 21st century. So we are talking about right-brain as well as left-brain skills because otherwise how can the manager think and act holistically? Managers (and it is fair to say, particularly male managers) have in the past been very much conditioned to left-brain thinking processes. Indeed management originated as a left-brain process.

We now need to introduce throughout the organisation the ability to think and sense intuitively and instinctively as well as rationally and logically. This is no less true for the management of risk than it is for mainstream management. Risk should be a positive consideration rather than negative, opportunity rather than threat. Creating such a culture will undoubtedly give a competitive edge on others in your sector or industry.

Let's give a specific example in the public sector. On the initiative of the finance director, there was a need to facilitate the process of identifying, understanding and reviewing the top risks in a major capital project. By definition, this project affected the whole organisation, its strategy and prospects for success. Although the exercise was simple and straightforward, it had a catalysing effect both inside and outside the organisation. Even after a few weeks, the Chief Executive discovered in casual conversation with industry peers "you appear to be light years ahead of us".

By now it is hoped that you are getting some clear insights into how to introduce and sustain the management of risk in the mainstream of management and business processes in your organisation. The skills to be learned or developed include:

➤  awareness and an enquiring mind;

➤  communication skills and how to facilitate learning and understanding;

➤  holistic thinking, integrating both the right and left brain across the organisation and ideally in individuals;

➤  quality management, learning by experience and understanding the importance of the continuous cycle of improvement;

➤  financial, commercial and general business awareness;

➤  knowledge and understanding of the organisation.

We have listed just a selection above and you may already have noticed the similarity with broader management skills. This is the point; management with awareness of risk should become an integrated part of the mainstream management processes.

In addition to these, it will of course be of value to have some people in the organisation with a specific understanding and/or the ability to think and focus on the management of risk. It does not matter if at the outset you do not have the skills or experience in the organisation. Carefully selected, bringing in the right consultant or advisor on a short-term basis as a 'resident risk manager' can act as the desired catalyst. Usually someone will emerge or the organisation will determine the manager or managers most appropriate to lead and take risk forward.

So how can these skills be refined, developed, taught or learned? As we said earlier, apart from this text and one or two others in the marketplace there is still a dearth of references on the management of risk. Also, among those that do exist, there is a strong bias towards the financial management of risk and an element of prescription. Of course you want the organisation to have the management of risk and control processes and procedures to ensure that risks to the long-term value of the organisation are identified and the steps are taken to eliminate or manage them as appropriate.

A very good way forward is to take those who have been identified to lead the process of managing risk and either second them or otherwise get them to meet organisations which are already skilled and experienced in this field.

We are not talking about rocket science here. (Although financial engineering is often compared as such.) The challenge for many organisations often appears to be what comes first? Should you establish a strategy and an action plan and then get some training? Should you get the training first before deciding on whom to train and in what skills?

Clearly it is important to see the whole process of establishing training and education within the overall framework and structure for managing risk

# 14

# Risk  Process  (Structure)

Implicit throughout this book is an acceptance of the importance of clearly defined management and business processes in the organisation. This would also be true for the risk process, except that we would expect these eventually to be integrated into the overall management processes.

Among the key questions here would be:

> Is there a formally recognised structure enabling risk to be identified at every stage of the management process from strategy through to implementation?

> Is it more appropriate for the organisation to have an in-house or external risk consultant - at least in the early stages of the process?

> Who actually has the necessary experience of risk awareness and/or the management of risk in the organisation?

What is essential, is the creation of an easily recognised structure or set of processes throughout the organisation that is capable of continual enhancement reflecting the emerging lessons from the other seven identified key elements.

These processes would include:

> Monitoring of risks identified and actions taken accordingly;

> Links with the business planning process and budgets;

➢   Links to other specific disciplines, e.g. Project Management, learning from, contributing to them and involving them within the organisation's management of risk processes.

It is an important decision as to whether to outsource the management of risk or not. This is not just dependent on the size and/or affordability of the organisation. It will also depend on the existing set of skills and the openness to change, as well as the organisation's maturity in relation to risk. An additional factor would be where there is one or more significant projects going on.

Project management is the management of risk at every stage of the process. The lessons learned and the understanding gained through the risk evaluation and consequent decisions in relation to projects are widely used for the whole organisation. A growing number of organisations are finding that mainstream operational management is very much about project management. The techniques, disciplines and experience of project management give a good insight into risks and how to manage them and are readily transferable back into the core operations.

Where the organisation goes outside for risk advice, the extent of any service provided should depend much more on the organisation's maturity and readiness for change than the budget it is prepared to make available for the task. Risk advisors are nowadays involved in all the strategic aspects, disciplines and processes of a wide variety of organisations, and sectors and industries. Most of this experience is readily transferable and can help enormously to flatten the organisation's learning curve. It is not how much you pay, but more, what you are getting for the money

The degree of use of external advisors will of course also depend on the extent of the availability of the internal ability – its relevant experience, core competencies and a readiness to learn and change. Increasingly, organisations are outsourcing additional services that are required rather than creating a de facto function for the management of risk. This is especially true in a low-value and high-volume business. There is of course a need to retain in-house supervision.

You might want to ask yourself whether managing risk is about direction or co-ordination of the appropriate resources and processes? Among the obvious aspects to consider for outsourcing are the time consuming areas such as claims handling and audit, in order to free-up a risk manager's time to concentrate on the bigger picture and the strategic view.

Where you go outside the organisation for the provision of a full service for the management of risk, you should ideally be seeking the 'holistic' approach. There must be a question whether any one organisation has all the skills necessary or indeed if they had, if this dependence would actually meet your needs.

In addition, while insurance experience or background is of undeniable value, you will very quickly determine whether an insurance-based approach is being offered. Insurance questionnaires are still retitled as risk questionnaires. Insurance is just one of the many avenues which you can choose to go down in the management or control of risk.

Starting out with an insurance mentality may protect you from the financial consequences when things go wrong, whether planned or unplanned. For two reasons at least, we advocate a different approach. First, it must be better to plan for and avoid the eventuality happening in the first place, rather than satisfy yourself with a financial pay out while the business continuity or momentum is lost.

Second, by managing with an awareness and understanding of risk not only of the potential events that can lead to loss or other damage. Also from the positive, opportunistic attitude that decisions are being made having taken account of all possibilities, you will have a significant lead over most of your peers or competitors.

The organisation needs to have an appropriate process that meets its (increasing) needs for managing risk. The process should of course mirror the management and reporting structure and it goes without saying that it needs to be wide ranging. It should follow the organisation's structure, being incorporated within the overall management and business processes.

The structure needs to enable rather than inhibit the corporate and risk strategy, the planning and implementation, and continuous improvement processes.

Returning to the analogy between the corporate mind and the human mind. If we were to adopt a negative or defensive management of risk strategy in our everyday lives, not only would we have never achieved or experienced many of life's most worthwhile objectives or occasions, but we might also never have set foot outside the front door.

Take the every day example of driving a car. Why insure the car? Not just because the law requires you to because in that case you might take only third party insurance. You certainly don't insure the car with the expectation of collecting regular dividends on expenditure. All that would happen then is that you would lose your no-claims bonus and the premiums would rise inexorably.

When you buy a car and especially when you sit in it and drive it, you do not expect to be involved in accidents. Instead, you have learned driving skills with great diligence. You practise them to the best of your ability. Hopefully, when things go wrong: a traffic offence; or a near miss, these can be looked upon as learning experiences. Otherwise, matters could go rapidly downhill.

Driving a car has become a necessary utility in our daily business and personal lives. While driving with reasonable care and attention, we all seek to complete a journey as swiftly, safely and effectively as possible. Hopefully, we drive with an awareness of what is going on around us and in reasonable comfort. We may have taken a conscious decision to purchase comprehensive insurance to cover all reasonable eventualities, but that doesn't eliminate the need to proceed with conscious or unconscious awareness of risks at every stage, safely and effectively and making the most of them.

And so it is with business. You have determined where you want to get to and have mapped a route accordingly, in order to complete the journey as swiftly and effectively as possible. The organisation is insured, serviced and well maintained and has the necessary fuel (resources, especially people) to achieve your goal. As you proceed along your chosen route, various different challenges and opportunities present themselves. You rapidly understand and process them, adjusting your speed, direction and expectations accordingly.

Whether using traffic information services, or a sense of perception, conscious and unconscious processes of awareness and appropriate adjustment, you will all the while be taking account of the risks and challenges and taking them in your stride as you proceed towards your chosen goal. Tomorrow, you will successfully complete other journeys.

Taking the analogy between the corporate mind and the motor car just one step further, while there is one person who drives at any one time, it can be shared among the other members of the team. Meanwhile, electronic and mechanical systems and processes in the car and the management and business processes and supporting systems in the corporation run smoothly and effectively.

While there are many mechanical aspects to managing a routine business, in the present day environment it is increasingly important that holistic awareness and understanding and creative and lateral thinking processes are brought to bear. Leading edge organisations are increasingly valuing instinct and intuition. We need to listen to the sound of the engine.

Innovation and originality are fundamental. Intel, the world's largest suppliers of microchips expect that in a year's time 90% of products they are selling will not have been designed or invented yet.

If you want to, you can be restrained by a mechanistic, traditional and often outdated method of management. Alternatively, you can encourage originality and more right-brain approaches.

People very often talk about wanting more control in their own lives. Some of the highest achievers in business and personal life have discovered that the best way is by letting go. Empowerment is not just another passing fad invented by Rosabeth Moss Kanter. It is a way of life for managers and organisations in the rapidly changing, global, high-tech markets of the 21st century.

The very different, almost unique, approach to the management of risk that we advocate here, sets it firmly at the heart of holistic business management. Remember, this is not minimalism and defensiveness, but positivity, opportunity and optimisation. Using your own all-encompassing definition of the word manager, you will have your own method of consciously structuring management processes to achieve your corporate and individual aims.

➤        ➤        ➤

# 15

# Risk Recording

At each stage of the management processes, it is possible to identify and evaluate the relevant risks. The purpose of recording such risks, their possible consequences and a recommended course of action, is not mere bureaucracy but rather the opportunity to improve their awareness and understanding, ensuring that the organisation is managing by taking account of risk.

At each stage of the management process design we described earlier, i.e. direction, resources, implementation, measurement, improvement, we have the opportunity to ask the same sort of questions:

> ➤ What risk or risks do we identify in this stage of the process?
> ➤ What are the risks specific to each decision?
> ➤ What is the nature of each risk?
> ➤ What is the potential impact on resource requirements?
> ➤ What additional resource or changing disposition might be required to handle it?
> ➤ What is the probability of it happening?
> ➤ What is the potential impact of this risk?
> ➤ What potential benefits may flow from understanding or managing this risk?
> ➤ How and in what ways can we limit or remove this risk?
> ➤ What preparations or contingencies do we already have in place?

➤   What other limitations are there on our desired course of action?

➤   What are the overall net potential quantitative and qualitative consequences?

### Recording Processes and Systems

The processes need to be in place to ensure that risks are identified, captured as soon as possible thereafter, recorded and monitored, including the agreed course of action. Supported by a pro forma, all the above will be documented, approved including authorisation for the course of action and also will take account of who else needs to be informed. The documentation which should be produced, will summarise the key risks facing the business at every stage including the following information:

➤   A description of the risk;

➤   The potential impact of the risk on the organisation;

➤   The likelihood of the risk occurring;

➤   The person directly responsible for managing the risk;

➤   The existing controls;

➤   Actions required to reduce the risk;

➤   A timetable for action

And ideally, these processes will be supported by a risk database, preferably available to all through an Intranet. There are a number of proprietary software products or packages available that can help with the development of plans and processes.

➤      ➤      ➤

# 16

# Risk Handling

Risk handling is about the way the organisation deals with the risk both before and after the occurrence of incidents. It is primarily related to the way events are dealt with, as and when and after, they occur.

**Key questions here are:**
- How effective is the organisation in preparing for and handling risk incidents?
- Are the organisation's management processes and systems established to take account of risk incidents?
- Is there a clearly defined manual setting out planned and agreed policies and procedures?
- Has the process been documented?
- Is it widely understood and regularly tested or otherwise audited?
- Has the process been systematised, ideally supported by database?
- Are the opportunities for learning and wider understanding from such incidents being maximised?
- Are the opportunities for quantitative or qualitative gain from sound risk handling procedures being maximised?
- How confident are you that the associated costs are being minimised?

# *Incident Handling*

It should be clear from the foregoing that incident handling does not just start when an incident has occurred. We should stress again here that the ideal is proactive management of risk. Errors, mistakes and accidents will occur. This is the people factor in risk. The fundamental of sound management of risk is to minimise such risk through a holistic understanding and awareness of what risks are inherent in the organisation or business, combined with sound training and education and empowerment to optimise the potential consequences.

It starts with planning therefore. Scenario planning allows the organisation to consider all possible risks, determine the likely course of action in each case, and thereby prepare its risk handling plan and arrangements in advance of any possible incident. If nothing happens, all well and good. It may just be that through risk planning, the organisation is better able to reduce the probability of such incidents if not to minimise the consequences to the quality of service and long-term value.

In general, however, incident handling is the handling process once the incident has occurred. For example, 'claims' handling is the process once a claim is made against the organisation or made by the organisation, following an incident.

Loss handling is the process of either or both minimising the potential consequences of the incident and maximising the potential return from whatever insurance or other retention or recovery mechanism was put in place.

Just as important therefore is how does the organisation go about the process of handling risks (i.e. before a risk turns into loss)?

So we are making clear here the important distinction between incident handling and risk handling. The better prospect for the long-term optimum return is ensuring that the risk handling processes are in place before any incident may occur. At the macro level we may call this disaster and contingency planning.

### Returning to the Corporate and Individual Analogy

Within any environment a human being is continually making both conscious and subconscious decisions as to how they will react to a given set of circumstances in which they may be or are about to, become involved.

The resultant outcome will be dictated by the course of action (or inaction) followed. This will reflect the experiences gained from previous identical (or similar) events, subsequent outcomes and personal desires or expectations.

The methods developed by the human brain for handling these circumstances will vary depending on the extent to which it may be affected directly or indirectly, the level of protection, success or reward to be obtained and the perceived ability to act (or respond).

The differences for the corporate body in handling the risks with which it is faced vary significantly from that of the human being except in taking its natural conscious and unconscious decisions. In this respect, we are reminded again of the people Risk Factor.

The corporate body, despite its own particular organisational structure does actually consist of a number of individuals. Each with their own experiences, desires, backgrounds and knowledge base.

You may believe that the organisation has been conditioned to anticipate and manage risk well in the event that it occurs. Unfortunately, at the end of the day you are still dependent on individuals, their own conditioning and human fallibility. It is for this reason alone that you need processes of separation and control in key areas of the business. This was one of the factors apparently missing at Barings Bank.

In addition, there are the written and unwritten rules and protocols of business, governmental influences, legal constraints, 'market' conditions, competitor responses etc. all of which will at varying times and in differing sets of circumstances create the need for a 'group' decision to be taken.

For this to be achieved three things tend to happen: relevant and essential supporting information is required; time elapses; and discussions take place. With the luxury of time available, the organisation may come to the right decisions (that is, the optimum in the circumstances).

Very often in practice, however, incidents happen suddenly and without warning. Especially in empowered organisations, individuals feel the need to make rapid decisions. They do not always remember the importance of consultation or even communication to other affected parties. It is at these times that an organisation needs the trust that:

> ➤ sound objective management of risk is part of the culture;
> ➤ that it is integrated into management processes;
> ➤ that the people concerned have the right skills and experience to make objective decisions (supported by the right training and education); and
> ➤ that the best risk recording and handling systems are in place.

# 17

# Risk Assurance (Audit & Compliance)

In the last few years there has been a natural convergence between management of risk, audit and compliance. 30 years ago audit was very much a matter of verifying the accuracy of transactions and assuring them that the accounts showed a true and fair view of the organisation's performance during the year and its value at the year end.

The greater pace and complexity of even the public sector, together with the massive growth in legislation and regulation meant that it wasn't long before audit and inspection had to become more focussed. Starting with the introduction of statistical methods, a risk-based approach was rapidly adopted.

During the same period, there has also been an exponential growth in national and international accounting standards. This has not only reflected the growing complexity of organisations and their reporting, but also the need to provide common and where possible, benchmark measures of performance.

Auditors are not only required to report on the historical performance, they are also expected to be aware of and have a view of risks inherent in the business at the time of reporting, together with in the immediately foreseeable future. Where this process has broken down, there has been a growing practice of litigation against auditors.

As far as internal audit is concerned, this has also moved away from a routine inspection type approach and towards management of risk and the reinforcing of quality management processes and the continuous cycle of improvement.

Some organisations have even gone as far as introducing internal management consultancy. We now see the logic in all these functions converging with management of risk.

The simple, standard review model proposed is as follows:

➤ Specifically how well have we performed during the period under review?

➤ Where and in what ways could we improve our performance?

➤ Overall how well did we do in the context of long-term goals and objectives?

In the optimum scheme of things, it should not be necessary to have both an audit department and separate management of risk function. Internal audit has moved beyond the days of historical checking. Where an incident has occurred, which results in loss or under performance or a breakdown in overall planned efficiency and service, there was clearly an inherent risk. Three questions that could be asked therefore are:

➤ Assuming we have a sound management of risk planning and implementation process, how could this incident have occurred?

➤ What lessons can we learn from this incident, which can improve our overall capability to optimise performance, sustain value and achieve objectives?

➤ What actions do we want to take as a result of this incident, including any improvements that can be made to the management of risk processes overall?

## The Components

Risk assurance has two important components:

➤ How can we be assured that we have adequate risk planning and management arrangements in place to anticipate the possibility of and manage for risks?

➤ Through what policies, processes, procedures and e.g. handling arrangements can we minimise the consequences of incidents where they occur?

In terms of practical questions, you should want to know:

➤ Has an audit been completed within the previous twelve months?

➤ Did this audit include a specific audit of risk and its management processes?

➤ What is the relationship between the audit function and the management of risk process?

➤ Are risk processes and supporting systems (including documentation and database where appropriate) sufficient to ensure that risk is anticipated, that incidents are picked up and recorded where they occur and that the appropriate actions follow, including business and financial recovery where provided for?

## The Role of Audit

It is an unnecessary inefficiency to keep audit and the management of risk completely separate. Apart from the obvious possibility of gaps and overlaps between the two functions, there is no useful purpose in separating the review of all that went wrong from the planning and implementation processes intended to minimise the possibility in the first place. As with the overall management process described earlier (DRIMI), it should be cyclical. In a relay race, the more people that handle the baton the greater the risk that it will be dropped.

Apart from internal audit and the management of risk being integrated or at least working in seamless harmony, a clear partnership between these functions and the external auditor will be of more cost effective and greater overall value to the organisation in the continuous improvement process.

That is the key point. The management of risk and audit should both be about assured delivery of objectives and sustained long-term value creation, together with facilitating and informing a continuous cycle improvement.

Until the mid-1980's very few organisations had Audit Committees. Even now, they are often seen as a mechanism for supervising the internal and external audit processes. We would see no net value to the organisation in separating the function of the Audit Committee from an overview of risk at the strategic level. Certainly, in the case of a financial organisation there is an argument in favour of having an ALCO (Asset/Liability Committee), not only because of the highly specialised nature of financial engineering and balance sheet management.

The Board and its sub committees are responsible for approval and review of strategic plans. Management is responsible for preparing such plans, recommending them to the Board, ensuring their implementation, measuring their success, determining potential improvements and accounting for the whole. Management is responsible for the same, integrated processes of managing risk.

Audit Committees have become somewhat synonymous with corporate governance. It should be remembered, of course, that the Board cannot delegate its ultimate accountability to a committee. The Board (or other supervising authority in the public sector) is the medium for corporate governance. Governance is not just about satisfying rules and regulations; it is also about ethics, creation and protection of long-term value, understanding and meeting of all stakeholder interests, etc.

It could even be said that in those organisations where governance has been introduced as a set of routines as opposed to explicit evidence of the thinking, understanding organisation, that overall risk may thereby be increased rather than reduced. Slavish dependence on routine tends to stultify original thinking. It is the objective use of initiative and intuition in the context of the agreed strategic direction and a known, understood holistic set of risks, which may be the keystone in differential performance.

# The Role of Benchmarking

What we are implying here is that the management of risk and risk assurance is about setting and meeting benchmarks at every stage of the process. Benchmarking those things that have to be done against internal and external best practice, constantly seeking ways to better understand and improve, ensuring the wide dissipation, understanding and ownership of the whole process of managing risk.

Having put in place a carefully crafted strategic plan for the management of risk you will want to be sure of the extent of progress in line with those plans. This is particularly true of any legal implications or those of best practice as measured or indicated by the market place that you operate within.

Assurance is just that, the process by which the confirmation is confidently delivered by way of continual 'audit' in an easily understood way and which allows progress to be independently and systematically verified. This promotes progress (often including to those in the outside world).

Of course, what is also required is the ability of those carrying out the audit process to actually have some understanding of what risk is and its implications on the organisation. To do this it needs to be much more than a tick-box exercise. It also requires the promotion of and the ability to 'spot' risk

Let us return to the corporate/human analogy. Not many people run their lives with the daily expectation that things will go wrong. If they did, they would take appropriate steps such as staying at home. So how do we all manage when there are risks all around us from the moment we are born?

Well over 95% of our processing takes place unconsciously. (In addition, by the way, we rarely use more than five per cent of our brain capacity.) We talked earlier of the process of learning from unconscious incompetence to unconscious competence. That is the route to follow. Individuals and managers usually have sound instincts when they are trained, encouraged and empowered to use them in the context of the overall plan.

The first question therefore is, is everyone aware of the organisation's aims, objectives and plans? Throughout our lives unfortunate incidents sometimes occurred often without warning. When they did, they caused us actual or psychological pain or discomfort. The human organism is genetically designed to learn. That's how we got where we are. In the meanwhile, where we allow ourselves to be aware we get constant positive feedback about what is going right for us. Every variation from plan is an opportunity to learn.

So why should the condition for human beings in organisations be fundamentally different from the circumstances in every day life? It is asking individuals to restrict their natural instincts and ability and become practised in defensive thinking or routines that inhibit enterprise. Of course, we are not talking about total freedom. Rather as with membership of any sporting team, there is an expectation that they will express that individual capability while taking account of a responsibility to the group.

The most productive assurance in everyday life comes from positive feedback and a constructive facilitation of the opportunity to learn. Keep telling people what they are doing wrong and you might produce a culture which either discourages initiative or leaves people too nervous to try and do what is best. One of the best and most successful training or learning techniques is role-playing. People can learn in practice the rules, but the best way forward is through experiential understanding.

This does not mean to imply that we are encouraging or tolerating mistake or error. It does mean that you have pre-planned the possibility of incident, rehearsed the choice of actions, and look on actual incidents as learning opportunities.

In a positive culture of managing risk, therefore, risk assurance is an assurance that things are going right with growth through learning, rather than an assurance that things are not going wrong and the stifling of initiative and enterprise. Of course this takes a new style of management, but do you want your organisation or corporation to be a leader or a follower, a success or also-ran?

When we examine our own experience of life and those around us, we have seen all too much of the culture of blame. It has become a national disease in the UK, whereas in the US there is a more successful economic model based on the culture of enterprise and opportunity.

We must question the value of a culture of blame and no-blame in any organisation. Many people talk the no-blame culture, that is until something of importance goes wrong, amiss or awry. Then far too often in the past the cold hand of blame and retribution has landed heavily on those accused of the incident.

In western society, people all too often look for somebody else to blame when things go wrong. Let us change that to a culture where we all professionally and objectively manage to plan for risk and its potential consequences. Not by way of expectation but much more to minimise probability and impact and to optimise the raft of opportunities that flows from such a broad and deep understanding of the elements of our business. We should see every occasion when things go wrong as an opportunity to learn and grow in the continuous cycle of improvement.

In this context, the management of risk and audit can combine to assure stakeholders and yourselves that you are doing at least as well as you planned rather than worse than you hoped.

# 18

# Risk Management & Governance

So let us return to the subject of governance, because much of the impetus towards professional management of risk in the 1990's has come from the regulatory and governance industry, which arose largely as a result of spectacular corporate failure.

Ultimately, the management of risk is the responsibility of the Board. The Board as the government's medium of the organisation, approves and oversees strategy and policy.

At the strategic level, some of the questions and issues that arise are:

➤ What is risk in the context of our business organisation?

➤ Managing risk - what is it and what does it imply for our management processes?

➤ Where does responsibility for the management of risk reside?

➤ Why should we manage risk?

➤ What are the benefits of managing risk?

➤ Name eight corporate risk-handling techniques?

➤ Do we comply with legislation, good practice, standards and regulation of governance?

We believe that the Risk Factor approach marks a watershed between the old insurance and governance driven management of risk and a new, positive, opportunistic style. This style will be integrated into the strategic plan and management processes, operating with a planned and considered evaluation of all relevant risks at every stage. In a fast moving, global competitive marketplace, this opportunistic approach can both create and sustain long-term value.

Some might go as far as to ask the question "has the management of risk and governance as we knew it had its day?" Certainly there are new challenges for regulators, boards of directors, auditors and management alike. People creating, working and implementing at the sharp end of the business will not be responsive to a process that tells them they can't do things. This goes against the grain of empowerment.

Instead, the whole organisation needs to operate in a climate where decisions are made rapidly and effectively while risk and its consequences are planned for, considered, assessed, evaluated, understood and taken account of without slowing the momentum of progress.

## *The Historical Perspective of Governance*

### The Turnbull Report (UK)
This laid down expectations of a sound system of internal control to safeguard shareholders' interests and the corporation's assets. It is a code of guidance on corporate governance for directors of listed companies.

There are three Guiding Principles:

1) That the Board should maintain a sound system of internal control to safeguard shareholders' investment and the company's assets;

2) That the directors should at least annually conduct a review of the effectiveness of the organisation's system of internal controls and should report to shareholders that this has been done. The review should include:

> Financial;
> Operational;
> Compliance Controls; and
> The management of risk.

3)   Companies that do not have an internal audit section should from time to time review the need for one.

Therefore, according to Turnbull, internal control is one of the principal elements, as is the transfer of risk to third parties, the avoidance of unplanned risk-taking, contingency planning and the sharing of risks through joint ventures.

## The Cadbury Report 1992

This was the first formal recommendation on Corporate Governance. It established a Code of Practice. Internal Controls should be designed to limit exposure to financial loss.

It also stressed the importance of the role of Non-Executive Directors, reporting on the effectiveness of internal financial controls.

## The Greenbury Report

Focused on executive remuneration packages.

## The Hampel Report 1998

Reviewed the impact of the Cadbury Report and added its own recommendations.

In truth, Cadbury was not widely acknowledged and accepted, even though its recommendations were built into company management and reporting expectations. In some senses, it led to a fairly mechanistic observance. This is not in keeping with the fast-changing global economy in which we operate. Even the public sector is progressively opening up to competitive forces, especially through outsourcing and the introduction of corporate capital.

Furthermore, commercial type management and reporting standards are being incorporated into best practice in the public sector also. Turnbull takes us a major step forward in facilitating a proactive, positive style of management of risk, rather than a negative, defensive, somewhat restrictive approach after Cadbury, which would only have been swept away by global forces and Internet based operations.

# *Integrating Risk into a New Way of Governance*

Being in business means taking risks. The successful organisation understands and manages risk effectively. Working in a positive, opportunistic manner it can continue to create and safeguard long-term shareholder value by being consciously and intuitively aware of the mix of positive and negative consequences of a range of different possible courses of action.

Of course, it's all very well theorising but it's the practical application that makes the difference. This is as true of managing risk as it is of any other managerial activity. Indeed any 'manager' who goes by that title is practically and implicitly, whether consciously or unconsciously, continually managing risk.

When you ask yourself the question, you have probably been aware of the issue of managing risk for at least the past 10 years. What we are giving to you in this book is a practical systematised approach to the handling of risk to achieve better, more sustainable returns without greater or worse consequences.

So maybe you have read the theory but find difficulty in seeing or recognising the benefits? We don't believe that there is anything revolutionary within the covers of this book, indeed some of you may have heard it all before.

However what this is about is the implementation of a holistic, open and aware risk culture combined with a practical systematised procedure and framework designed to actually deliver the results you want from your organisation's handling of risk.

Despite the publication of reams of documentation, much based upon theory, personal experience, second-hand knowledge, recommendations and regulations on governance and a substantial amount based around the financial management of risk, the question could fairly be asked as to the success of the management of risk so far. It is a rapidly changing picture, however.

Although it is not hitting the headlines in the press or being discussed much beyond the professional journals, over and over again we are finding that our calls in both the corporate and the public sector are getting an immediate positive response. Some of the most interesting examples are from the public sector.

With the growth of litigation, clinical governance has suddenly become a major concern for the UK health service. Risk is of course an ever-present factor, especially at the sharp end of patient treatment. Previously of course, personal accident and liability had been insured. Now the NHS has moved to a pooling arrangement that unfortunately has coincided with the rapid growth in claims.

Also in the NHS, there are a substantial number of capital projects financed by the private sector. New commercial arrangements and partnerships such as these bring an entirely new set of risks. The authors reviewed the risks in a massive new hospital development programme in Scotland. The trust concerned, one of the more go-ahead in the United Kingdom, wanted to use this exercise as the proving ground on which to build a longer term relationship around the management of risk. This would cover not only clinical governance but also holistic risk throughout the organisation.

One of the most significant messages to come from this exercise was that the Chief Executive wanted above all a positive approach to the management of risk. This was indeed music to our ears.

The subject of managing risk appears for many to remain shrouded if not in cloud then certainly it's surrounded by a thick haze. The Turnbull Report on Corporate Governance has propelled the management of risk up the agenda not only of listed companies, but also for other corporate and public sector organisations. After the Cadbury report was written in the early 1990's, the public sector moved forward just as much as many corporate sector organisations in implementing its recommendations on corporate governance.

The long awaited Turnbull report requires organisations to publish details of the risks they face and how the directors intend to manage these risks. From 2000, the annual reports of such organisations will be required to detail such risk-related activity by demonstrating the approach that the company has adopted and the issues that they have encountered on the way.

With such a prescriptive approach already being applied, we believe now is the time for organisations to move towards a wider, proactive management of risk approach which takes account of the practical requirements and considerations of legislation, regulation and best practice recommendation. But much more than that, to go beyond the structured, policy-led approach to one that embraces risk positively and opportunistically, to create competitive advantage.

In the wider public sector, the Audit Commission has made it clear that the management of risk should be an integral part of a Local Authority's overall management plan. Within the Health Sector the NHS has been taking seriously the issue of Corporate Governance with a dedicated department. Whether in the public or corporate sector, no one is going to penalise you if you adopt best practice as a foundation and go one step beyond towards benchmarked performance and achievement.

$$\succ \qquad \succ \qquad \succ$$

# 19

# Risk Integration

The management of risk requires a structured approach so that eventually all risks will be identified. In reality risk changes continually. New risks evolve and old ones reappear, sometimes in a new guise. Processes continue to develop in response to the market in which the organisation operates.

Sound, proactive management of risk is fundamental to the long-term survival of a business and should also enhance the value of the organisation. What we are looking at here is reducing risks through their sensible management. We do of course need to consider carefully the impact of losses on the organisation's profitability.

Insurance should become over a period of time the second medium as a financial safety net. In a sense we are talking about self insurance where you can consider funding and the development of streams of 'income' to support the ongoing day to day need for funds to 'settle' unplanned losses, as and when they arise.

The question is, can the body corporate and the individual be protected from loss or the potential for a loss with its associated costs whatever happens? The answer of course is no. In the old days we would have readily taken recourse to insurance. Despite competition in that sector also, when taking account of the costs of intermediation, insurance is not cheap. In the longer term, apart from those specialist risks or Acts of God that are beyond our control, we can no longer afford blanket insurance as an alternative to sound, objective management of risk.

Remember; at the end of the day insurance is a bet. It is based on past statistical patterns and predictions of probability. Given the number of intermediates between you and the ultimate underwriter of the risk, for any of your mainstream activities sound management of risk integrated into your day management processes must represent a better bet.

In the same vein, Corporate Governance should not be seen as an extra set of procedures to satisfy the stock exchange, regulators, auditing and reporting standards or what have you. We can neither afford nor does it enhance the understanding, empowerment, learning capability or potential for continuous improvement of the organisation when we slavishly follow structure and routine.

Of course corporate governance procedures should be seen as serving to protect the organisation, but surely protection is not what we are in business for?

Did we ever need the rules and regulations of corporate governance? Do we need risk managers? Or should we be capable of leading and managing our own organisations and corporations in the highest standards of self-regulation and self-determination where protection and enhancement of long-term value is the automatic by-product.

Should the management of risk be made compulsory? We believe no, because it creates the wrong mindset. Should the Government become involved? They already are via various initiatives, co-ordinating bodies, through policy laid down and by their implicit or explicit acceptance of auditing and reporting standards. Wherever you look, you will see government or quasi government bodies implementing or enforcing the same governance and reporting standards as the corporate sector.

### Managing Risk is a Skill

Traditional management of risk sometimes felt more like an imposition. Positive, proactive management of risk is a skill like any other management skill. It can be learned. The question and the reason for this book, is why:

> ➤ Its importance appears to have been underestimated by so many organisations?

> ➤ So many executives, senior managers and employees as well as customers, partners and other stakeholders misunderstand its relevance?

➤    There is so much confusion as to the extent of the topic?

➤    The subject appears to be fragmenting into self-interest topics?

➤    So many articles on the subject are product or services-led by those with an interest in promoting their own view or approach?

➤    Everyone wants to lay claim to the management of risk as theirs?

The skill of managing risk, like other management disciplines, needs to be an ongoing, developing one if it is to be effective.

On the one hand it appears to be gaining increasing acknowledgement, particularly by senior personnel within major organisations. This in the main seems to be brought about as much by a recognition of 'best practice' (albeit sometimes grudgingly) as it does by the understanding of the inextricable but under-appreciated links to every other management process in the organisation.

There are many excellent books available on an incredibly wide range of specialist topics listed under the headings of managing risk. A visit to the Internet will provide even more ammunition to anybody wanting to tackle this subject matter within their business.

It has been said that Risk Managers are not afforded the respect they deserve - why is this? Managing risk is an important activity for all organisations whatever the type of business, size or complexity. Some may see increasingly advanced technology as a threat but it is also the basis for dramatically improved possibilities for supporting and managing the business including in the field of managing risk.

Stated policy and actual practice are often poles apart. Where there is a risk manager, they are often working in isolation with little or no real influence on the departments with whom they should be interfacing as part of an integrated approach. In addition, they are also often without access to decision-makers and with little or no independent budget.

Organisations need to make the choice: are they going to have a formal function for the management of risk or are they going to integrate the management of risk into the management processes; or are they going to ignore risk altogether (apart from insurance)?

➤         ➤         ➤

# PART D

# Practical Experience of The Risk Factor

# 20

# Quality - the Risk Factor in Management Processes

By now it will be clear, that we advocate very much a constructively questioning and challenging approach to risk management, not as a stand-alone function but integrated into the daily management processes. Whilst at the outset people may ask the question 'what are the risks here?' when the process has become mature we would expect very much an implicit review of the issues that are present and the potential consequences.

A TQM orientation is one of the fundamentals of future success, alongside a clear and regularly reviewed strategic plan, a synergistic team and wider organisation and the ongoing implicit or explicit review of the Risk Factors. Embedded within a continuous cycle of improvement this is very much a qualitative approach to balance the quantitative value added, value creation process.

Becoming part of the routine, the hard and soft risks and their interrelation will be constantly evaluated through and integrated with a VAR (Value at Risk) approach. Management solutions to business risk will be viewed in a positive, constructive, opportunistic light. Understanding will be enhanced through adaptable, interactive management information systems, constantly updated to match the evolving organisation and including draw down and enquiry facilities. We recommend that a version of the risk matrix is incorporated within this both overall, and where appropriate to specific initiatives or functions.

This approach will enable the organisation to better understand and instinctively manage for the implicit risks. They will thereby reduce their likelihood and impact enabling the avoidance or diversion of risk where appropriate, transferring (spreading) risk through commercial, financial and insurance markets; retaining risk or making it work for you. In the end it all comes back to holistic and detailed understanding and that means more questions.

A quality management approach is fundamental and the explicit and implicit review of Risk Factors is complementary. Its implementation and sustenance is through the management and business processes. Understanding of Risk Factors enables objective quality decisions. Remember, we are not just talking about quantitative analysis here.

Any review of potential benefits is ideally complemented by a consideration of events that might limit the delivery of, or detract from, such benefits. In the short, medium and long-term you may be looking for solutions, for there is no longer any certainty, if indeed there ever was. Any solution will benefit from a review of the potential consequences especially when this is integrated into the management processes on an ongoing basis.

Policy and procedures often complement, and should not hold back, objective management processes designed and redesigned to implement strategic plans. While there may be risks in not having agreed and detailed policy and procedures, there are equally risks in these not being fully thought through and re-evaluated from time to time.

While in the mature organisation we do not see the need for a risk management function (indeed we are concerned about the possibility of it disappearing into a separate box), we would expect consideration of risk to sit alongside and be integrated with quality management processes. The role of the Risk Manager; while having value at the outset in focussing everyone in the organisation on its importance and relevance, should eventually be absorbed into the management processes. Indeed, even while there is felt to be a need for a role it can be and is increasingly effected from outside the organisation. It is the approach that we often adopt.

In the way that we contemplate risk management, the ideal reporting line for the risk manager is direct to the Chief Executive or managing director (or equivalent to, that is). In due course, it should be recognised that the instinctive understanding and consideration of risk is part of Directors' and Business Managers' responsibilities.

We cannot stress too much the importance of information and communication. Many organisations believe that they have excellent information and communication processes. Very often these include carefully developed briefing routines, both internally and externally. Communication is never effective, however, unless it is actually received by the right people and understood including its context.

Inside the organisation, it is desirable to have a communications audit process. Communication is often based around a top down process, implicitly or explicitly encouraging bottom-up feedback. In our experience the message may often be neither received properly nor understood. By regularly and randomly checking with the intended recipients it is possible not only to verify the effectiveness of the process but also to modify it to make it work more effectively.

## Risk Tolerance and the Risk Evaluation Process

Looked at in quantitative or qualitative terms, organisations may have a finite risk tolerance and especially where relevant to the business (e.g. financial services), specific risk limits. We can use the traditional risk management elements here:

- ➤  Determine the risk;
- ➤  Analyse the risk;
- ➤  Evaluate the risk;
- ➤  Manage the risk;
- ➤  Ignore it;
- ➤  Insure it;
- ➤  Control it;
- ➤  Improve the management and business processes or other environmental factors that represent the basis of the risk.

There are several books on risk management and many organisations still promoting traditional risk management techniques. By now you will have realised that our approach is very different. Particularly in production processes, risk control systems may be entirely appropriate.

As far as the overall methodology is concerned:

➤   Identify and assess the risk potential and the circumstances in which it may occur;

➤   Set the risk policies;

➤   Implement the risk policies;

➤   Manage the risks as appropriate;

➤   Monitoring and reporting;

➤   Testing and contingency plans (where appropriate);

➤   Documentation.

Risk management like mainstream management is very much a matter of circumstances and solutions; opportunities and threats; protecting assets and the viability of the business.

## A Quality Case Study

N&P underwent a great deal of change between 1982 and its merger with the Abbey National in the late 1990s. It was the product of a merger between two of the biggest building societies in the industry in 1982. This was not a quality process, the resulting organisation ending up with three cultures and three information systems. This was the situation in late 1985.

At the end of 1986, the Chief Executive retired due to ill health. During the interregnum, the acting Chief Executive was asked to lead a strategic planning process. A corporate mission was developed that survived to the end of N&P's days as an independent organisation. A new Chief Executive was appointed who only lasted two years. Eventually, David O'Brien, an existing non-executive Director was asked to take the reins.

David's extensive experience included running Rank Xerox UK. During this period, he was involved in developing leading edge management theory and practice, both for his employer and their clients. This included sophisticated business process reengineering, very much in the way that Hammer and Champey had originally intended.

He introduced this approach into N&P. It wasn't universally popular either inside or outside the organisation. Some managers left in disillusion and many outsiders couldn't understand the language or concepts of process-based quality management.

For obvious reasons, N&P was in some difficulty when O'Brien took over. It is fair to say that its prospects were transformed along with its methods of operation during his tenure. Unfortunately, this coincided with the continuation of the worst mortgage market in history. Quality management in every respect and process became a way of life. It was much admired by leading-edge thinkers and was cited as a case study in excellence. Still, it came in for some ridicule from N&P's competitors, the Leeds, with which they tried to merge.

Failure to consummate this marriage accelerated the decline in prospects and first O'Brien left, followed a year or so later by the merger with the Abbey.

It was however a good time for learning and being involved with the design and evolution of excellence in quality management. Regrettably, with limited capital resources, N&P eventually over reached itself. It was however a successful case study in the coexistence of quality and risk management evolving together to become part of the fabric of the strategic and operational processes. The lessons learned from that time, we have continued to apply in every aspect of our business lives. They have also been incorporated in this book.

# 21

# People & the Risk Factor

By now it may be clear that in adopting the approach we advocate, people become the Risk Factor. People are responsible for determining and leading the strategic direction. People are responsible for designing and implementing the processes. People are responsible for being explicitly or implicitly aware of potential risks and accountable for their consequences. In our experience, there isn't a single problem in the management of organisations, which isn't ultimately down to the decision of an individual or individuals. Consequently, coaching and developing people is a fast growing business.

What we want to advocate here is to create an empowering risk management culture. Empowerment implies a substantially greater degree of delegation of creativity and responsibility for decisions. It also involves a broader acceptance of accountability. This, in our experience, is one of the biggest single Risk Factors in the organisation. While accountability may be clear in the design of the organisation from the boardroom to the shop floor or the shop counter, it is far from clear in the minds of many of the people who are actually accountable. Indeed, when things go wrong as a result of anticipated risks, people often try to duck responsibility, let alone accountability.

It starts and ends with leadership. Leadership is the responsibility of the CEO (or managing director), supported by the CFO (or finance director). It has often been said that leadership cannot be learned or taught - that it is an innate quality. This does not in any way obviate the possibility of understanding exactly what leadership is about, what it implies, what it involves and what it looks like.

Leadership starts with individual leadership, self-determination, self-motivation and self-control. You may recognise these as essential components of emotional intelligence. Leadership is certainly needed when things go wrong and is more effectively employed in maximising the possibility of quality decisions and implementation from the outset.

Every person in the broader management team has individual responsibility for risk awareness, business decisions and management. Personnel management has grown up to be HR (Human Resources). (Unfortunately, some of the post holders have not evolved with the development from an operational to a strategic role). In leading the strategic importance of HR in the 21st century organisation, the HR director is responsible for advice, guidance and support in the strategic and operational management of the organisation. People risks are implicit at every stage.

Particularly in the public sector, there has been inconsistency in the step up from personnel management to HR. With people being the key Risk Factor, this is a major challenge to the organisation. In both the public and corporate sectors, the pace of change is accelerating and political, legal and regulatory requirements are growing. Strategic roles with a high operational content have become very complex. Introducing an empowering culture without commensurate strategic skills in the leadership of people is asking for problems.

The personnel Risk Factors alone are becoming ever more complex, especially as the practise of litigation grows. Every decision involving the management of an employee, runs the risk that it may later be cited in a court or tribunal. Executives and managers cannot be expected to understand all the ins and outs of personnel management. This is part of the policy function of the HR director. People management has become so important that it requires the full attention of the Chief Executive as well as the rest of the management team.

In the worst worlds, declining morale, growing levels of stress, high staff turnover, absence and sickness are just some aspects of the people Risk Factor. Management has the capacity to exacerbate as well as resolve potential difficulties. Even in the best worlds, in leading edge organisations where empowerment, innovation, creativity, personal growth and development, etc. are the norm, the challenges of change inside and outside the organisation are growing and becoming more complex. The process of outsourcing has often been driven by cost efficiency in the past. Now it may be encouraged by delegation of accountability for the people in individual processes.

Among the many aspects of the people Risk Factor are: corporate culture and morale; organisation structure, design and development; recruitment and termination; succession planning; training and development; rewards and motivation; and communication.

In the best organisations, directors and management are leading by example. There needs to be a clear allocation of responsibilities and transparent, enacted accountability. This is risk management at work in a very practical sense; Training and awareness, reduction in errors and an empowering process of self-appraisal and learning from mistakes are further elements. Openness of culture encourages openness of consideration and management of risks, as opposed to avoidance or ignorance.

There is still a widespread immaturity of people and organisations to the management of risk. It does not need to be taught as a separate subject but the way has be found to make it intrinsic and instinctive throughout the management and business processes.

➤    ➤    ➤

# 22

# The Risk Factor in Systems

First let us make clear the distinction between information technology and information systems. Information systems are the software and programmes that provide the data to support the management and business processes. Information technology is the hardware, communications network and other infrastructure on which the systems run.

It goes without saying that the Risk Factor in information systems is becoming ever more complex and diversified as the sources, uses and delivery mechanisms explode. We now live in a society that relies heavily on technology, often without thinking or realising. Take mobile phone technology for example. Apart from the fact that its sophistication and variety seem to grow daily, the understanding of all aspects and how to make optimum use of them is beyond many people. Converging with the hand-held computing device, these instruments can deliver a multiplicity of needs, many of which may not be drawn on by the majority of users.

These two examples are mentioned because their technology and systems are converging to the extent that sooner rather than later, many businesses may be capable of being substantially run from the hand, the home or the car. We have talked about it for so long but we already exist in the age of the virtual business. While business becomes virtual, risks remain real and they are not limited to the systems or the technology. Indeed, the majority of information related risks involve the use of and dependence on information.

Whether the information is wrong, unreliable or the system fails, in the fast moving complex global markets of the 21st century, such risks have the capacity to fundamentally undermine the quality of decisions and effectiveness of management and business processes. Again, consideration of the Risk Factors in information systems and technology could account for a book of its own. What is beyond doubt is that as their dependence on technology grows, every director has responsibility to understand IS/IT decisions being made, and their consequences. Above all, there is a need to be able to ask the right questions and have sufficient understanding to recognise an acceptable answer.

One doesn't need to be an expert to ask the simplest of questions, such as:

> ➤   what are the alternatives?
> ➤   what are the consequences?
> ➤   what are the costs and benefits in detail?; and above all,
> ➤   how will this decision create additional value or enhance the value creation process and at the very least avoid loss or damage, or inhibit it?

There are risks inherent in new technology, but there are of course also risks in retaining old technology. Unfortunately, the IT director's view of obsolescence may differ from that that of other members of the team, especially where expense is involved. Year 2000 was an interesting case study in itself. We may never know whether the risks were overblown because so much effort and resource was expended in avoiding the potential problems on a world-wide scale that we don't know to what extent they would have happened anyway. Nevertheless, it did encourage, force, or facilitate many organisations to update their technology and systems to the latest generation.

Year 2000 may have temporarily suspended the problem of legacy systems. This problem is particularly seen after mergers or take-overs.

In reflecting on systems risk, we also need to consider systems development risk. Many problems are caused where systems changes are effected, especially where these are unauthorised. Where there are multiple direct or indirect users of a system, software can be so complex that one apparently beneficial change for one user may have an unforeseen adverse effect on other users. It goes without saying that in the area of systems management there need to be high standards and visible controls, both documented and implemented (and regularly audited).

In particular, there needs to be wherever possible separation of function. So, the Risk Factors in information systems relate just as much to the design, procurement, implementation and change processes as they do to errors, systems failure and corruption. The consequences of failing to understand or manage these Risk Factors may extend far beyond process and business interruption, even to the point of business failure.

In the 1980s, a fire at Brunel university resulted in the loss of twelve years worth of irreplaceable information. Some projects probably never recovered. Daily, there are innumerable examples of businesses and organisations that have failed due to the failure of their information systems. We do not have the time or space to go into more detail here but the Risk Factors extend well beyond the obvious examples of: fraud; unauthorised access; malice; viruses; etc.

In a telecommunications and Internet driven and supported world, with the complementary growth of intranets and network computing, it could be said that we have become almost totally dependant on computing and interactive networks for most aspects of our business and personal lives.

The Risk Factor in information systems now extends to the lives and processes of all personnel. Systems support is now fundamental to the PC, mobile or hand-held of every individual. While failure of the technology has a potential nuisance value that extends as far as complete business failure, the vast majority of the risks are now related to the systems and programmes which actually run our business and daily lives.

The extraordinary and continuing decline in computing costs of the microchip, means that there is no excuse for not having security both on and off-site. While the continuity of business is certainly not helped by loss of or lack of key systems personnel, it has now become the responsibility of the individuals to achieve an understanding of the systems and technology on their desk and in their hand sufficient to deal with the day-to-day problems. Audit of systems and systems risk is now a fundamental requirement for organisations of any significant size but it can never be sufficient to handle the day-to-day challenges to management and business processes in a world which e.g. is now highly dependant on email and Internet processing.

➢       ➢       ➢

# 23

# Awareness of the Risk Factor

The learning process described earlier, progresses from unconscious incompetence to unconscious competence. Similarly with the risk awareness. Many organisations have, for some time had a conscious awareness of risk in their business. This would be especially true where risk was in the nature of their business, such as trading commodities, stock markets, etc.

It would be true to say however that most businesses and organisations have managed their daily routine with little more than an unconscious awareness of risk brought into mind from time to time by events, problems and losses. The evidence for this is in the relatively recent history of corporate governance.

## *Awareness, governance and control*

Organisations of any significant size that have to be audited would have an awareness of the importance of sound control. Many general managers or business leaders may well have had an instinctive or professionally based awareness, for instance trained accountants.

The escalation in the regulatory bodies and the whole growth of the corporate governance industry has largely been a testimony of insufficient self-regulation in both the corporate and public sectors. There have of course been many well publicised incidents.

Governance is largely about values. It's about the protection of stakeholder values, especially long-term value in the case of the corporate sector. We contend that instinctive or even conscious awareness and management of risk in its broadest most objective sense could have obviated the need for much of the governance panoply that has grown up.

### The future of regulation

We do not talk here about the regulation related, for example, to the utilities in the United Kingdom (e.g. gas, water, electricity, rail). Instead, we are referring e.g. to the financial services industry regulation but also implicitly to the tougher, more rigorous auditing standards being carried out.

It seems that whenever a highly visible example of corporate 'greed', incompetence or negligence is brought to the public eye, another piece of regulation, legislation or further content for the annual report seems to be the consequence.

The question is, whether this inexorable growth of governance can continue indefinitely? The biggest single threat is the Internet. When one looks at the growth of sophistication in service delivery and output, the explosion of material of a dubious content and the difficulty the authorities face in keeping track let alone policing it, one wonders about the consequences for governance.

As several slip-ups have already shown, it is possible for sensitive information to reach the public via the Internet much faster than through the traditional channels. We have become used to a diet of the annual, half yearly and sometimes quarterly reports from corporations. If it is becoming standard practise for intranets or indeed the Internet itself to be used for the internal publication of corporate progress, then how long before we have real time corporate publication of results?

Taken with the increase in short-termism, there may be a growing demand for up-to-the-minute information. Markets have become immensely more volatile and they feed on information or counter information. The problem is, it is difficult enough and takes such a long time to audit company reports at present. It cannot be too long therefore before a dichotomy exists between investors' hunger for information and the due process necessary to verify its accuracy and quality.

### Possible abandonment in favour of self-regulation

Whether deliberately or pragmatically therefore, we may begin to see the progressive dismantling of governance in favour of self-regulation. This may be especially true for global organisations. Already, annual reports are very out-of-date by the time they are read in this fast moving world. The Internet, sophistication of technology and simple security will increasingly challenge the ability to keep things tight until publication. Governance and audit themselves therefore may need to become more pragmatic.

National stock markets are now international. They rightly continue to seek to dissuade the purveyors of insider information. With the explosive growth of trading on the Internet, daily rumour and counter rumour, share prices savaged by profit warnings and the growing volatility of markets, the existing controls may be made redundant sooner rather than later. Furthermore, fundamental to the orderly progress of markets is the control or limitation of price sensitive information. As many events have shown, the definition of what is price sensitive is broadening daily mainly because of a proliferation of rumour and information on the Internet.

## Control Self-assessment

The growth of control self-assessment has been a very important development. None of what we say here should in any way undermine the responsibility and accountability of the owners, directors and managers of private and public sector organisations for sound management, ethical behaviour, sustained corporate values and development and protection in the interests of stakeholders.

So what about risk? From one point of view all these developments increase the risks to the organisation. Sound, adaptable, flexible management will see the opportunities to capitalise on these trends for the benefit of their organisations whilst remaining within probity. For other organisations, which are managing defensively or passively as opposed to managing with an awareness of the Risk Factors, there may be growing bureaucracy and infrastructure, tangible and intangible threats to the viability of the organisation.

## The Risk Awareness Process

Most professional sports teams would not consider taking the field without having thoroughly researched the opposition using some or all of the sophisticated technology available to them these days. The best, including such as Manchester United, have such confidence in their own ability and professionalism that as well as doing thorough preparation they also seek to impose their own patterns of play on the opposition.

And so with companies and organisations. Those with the culture which meant that they have drifted into governance late in the day with an uneven understanding of its demands and consequences, following bureaucratic rules and regulations can be expected to do relatively poorly. Their modus operandi is indicative of a defensive or responsive corporate mentality.

Those who are, and seek to remain, in control of their own destiny, will decide, implement and manage everything they do with an awareness of the Risk Factors. They will openly share much of the understanding both internally and externally, not fearing the opposition because of the lead they have over them.

We are talking about a completely new way of thinking for many organisations. Setting the goals and the outcomes, visualising their achievement and moving confidently towards success, all the while understanding the consequences of different courses of action and the basis for their chosen route.

Their objective and positive risk awareness will mean that they: plan for risk; prevent it as appropriate (minimise, transfer, or spread it); set their priorities accordingly; assess, audit, measure and monitor it. They will have early warning systems to give them the opportunity to reconsider and revise their course as appropriate.

# *Audit and the Management of Risk*

Our perception is that the best practise of both audit and risk management have come a very long way for the best organisations in the corporate and public sectors. It is fair to say that each sector has in different ways set a good example to the other from time to time.

Regrettably, many organisations still do not have an objective awareness of understanding and managing their business to the highest standards, constantly reviewing their performance and seeking to continually improve.

Awareness of the Risk Factors is not an awareness of a series of negatives. It is a positive constructive awareness of the factors that could inhibit the ultimate delivery of the highest possible standards together with those that pose a threat to the viability of the organisation. Managing these positively can create two competitive advantages.

First, there are many that would represent a threat to the whole sector let alone one organisation. Based on our experience, any organisation that proactively manages such threats will have a lead on many of their competitors. We refer once again to the Shell example earlier.

Second, a constructive, rational, objective review of the risks in the context of the opportunities and corporate goals, flexing and adapting as circumstances change, will lead to better holistic understanding and the optimum performance.

Many years ago, Sir Kenneth Cork used a set of ten indicators for companies facing bankruptcy. We would suggest that organisations that settle for market following behaviours and mediocrity in management will constantly under-perform their peers. Those that have reluctantly or tardily introduced governance and procedures for management of risk may well fall into this category.

Meanwhile, some leading edge organisations have already seen the value of merging internal audit and risk management in the nature of internal consultancy integrated into every management process of the organisation such that it becomes a core competency.

➤        ➤        ➤

# 24

# The Risk Factor in Minimising Cost, Adding & Protecting Value

Quantifying risks is a process normally related to organisations that are in the business of creating or supporting transactions in financial commodities. While our approach in this text has been more qualitative this does not obviate the possibility of putting a value on risk. Indeed, the basis of the simple assessment process referred to earlier (that is the top six risks, evaluated by probability and impact) does allow for an element of numerical benchmarking.

While quantifying the potential value of risks could be a worthwhile exercise in determining whether to insure a given risk or not, the Risk Factor based approach goes well beyond this.

The last ten years or so has seen the progressive growth of the use of corporate sector capital for public sector projects in the United Kingdom. Many have taken place under the PFI (Private Finance Initiative, now PPP or Private/Public Partnerships). The need arose through two factors in the UK Treasury: first, the finity of public sector funds, especially from 2010 onwards; and secondly, due to the Treasury practise of cash accounting, increasing difficulty of funding substantial capital investment out of what is essentially a revenue budget. PFI turns capital projects into annual streams of cost.

A downside is, that the corporate sector requires two returns that the public sector does not need: a profit margin; and compensation for taking the majority of risk. Consequently, whenever PFI projects are proposed there is a need to bring the value of risk transfer into the equation in order that the corporate sector proposal can show better value. The techniques being used for this risk assessment are highly sophisticated, drawing on e.g. Monte Carlo simulation methods. This is quantification of risk at its most complex. The reader will be reassured that we do not see the need for anything so complex in the Risk Factor based approach.

## *Value added approach*

What we're talking about here is choices and value added. Once we accept that corporate sector objectives are characterised by creating or sustaining long-term value, the Risk Factors become a key determinant in deciding between choices that can enhance or detract from such value.

In the public sector, once again, the context of the Risk Factors is their propensity to impact on performance objectives, service quality and value. It is a dangerous simplicity to dismiss the importance of valuing the public sector where the key financial driver is cost. So, the corporate sector objective to create long-term value becomes a public sector equivalent of protecting value through minimising cost to achieve the desired service and performance standards.

In both situations it becomes a matter of balancing facts and intuition. While this may be more so in the corporate sector, cost and the depth of the public purse are major factors in the public sector, especially where e.g. local taxes are the consequence of growth in spending.

### Risk Related Returns

We have seen the growth of VAR, EVA (Economic Value Added) and other measures of risk-adjusted returns. Even without going to the degree of sophistication of Modigliani and Miller and other mathematical models, we prefer to use quantified Risk Factors as a means for deciding between alternatives (when taken together we have more subjective or intangible factors), rather than as an outright measure of performance. The rapid growth in the use of benchmarks has been more associated with the advent of quality management than their usefulness for financial comparison.

Historical measures of performance are exactly that. By the time a corporation reports, its results may already be months out of date. When analysts have had a chance to compare different organisations with different accounting periods, the rapidly moving world will have already moved on. Increasingly, the US practice of evaluating organisations in terms of their cash generation capacity is being adopted in Europe. In rapidly changing global markets it is a much better measure of a company's viability than its price/earnings ratio.

We do see however, a potential value of using evaluated Risk Factors as a basis for the allocation of capital in business developments, investments and capital projects.

### The Value of Risk

So what is the value of risk? First of all, it is potentially transitory. It is changing and moving all the time. Even though performance objectives may be set in the future, their prior evaluation can only by definition be made on the basis of historical evidence. Neither the probability, nor the potential impact are certain. If they were, we would all have retired years ago as millionaires.

So while supporting the use of a financial evaluation of risks as an add-on to the process of setting objectives or deciding between different projects, our own approach is one of experientially and intuitively determining a broad, holistic range of Risk Factors inside and outside the organisation. They are then weighed against each other in determining the state of play and between different courses of action available at any one time.

Note, implicit in the above is an objective ongoing process of inquiry. As with strategic planning the best managers do not complete the exercise and then simply file it until the outcome before comparing actual performance with plan. Instead, continually observing and checking the various Risk Factors keeps progress under constant review adapting and flexing as the need arises. All the while, they are attuned to the corporate mind and to the rapidly changing markets in which they exist.

### The Cost of Risk

Despite our apparently subjective approach, it should be realised by now that we readily recognise risk as having an apparent or actual cost. This can be further sub-divided into: direct and indirect cost; losses, damage to or diminution of value; loss of expected benefits or opportunity cost of benefits foregone. All risks have a potential or actual cost. The trick is in balancing the cost of the management of risk against the evaluated potential consequences, constantly reassessing on an ongoing basis.

In the practical management of day-to-day risks, the decision may be between what to ignore, what to insure, what to control and manage. Many may see the practical cost of risk as being in: insurance; broking; underwriting; spreading the risk; specialist insurance; (even sometimes paying for unnecessary insurance, rather than evaluate or contemplate the risk). Whichever approach is adopted there is a need for assessment and constant monitoring and review.

The point we are trying to make here however is that in a world of long-term value creation: the opportunity costs on decisions, initiatives or projects which either weren't identified or followed for want of a Risk Factor based approach; or the lack of a broader Risk Factor based analysis of failed initiatives; may in the long run be more significant than the financial and business implications of losses avoided by taking a defensive stance.

Competitive advantage is transitory at best in the rapidly changing global markets. The time taken to conduct detailed financial evaluation of a range of alternatives will eat into any lead time there may be whether it is a new product or capital project. With the Risk Factor approach, management and directors constantly have their finger on the corporate pulse with an intuitive awareness of markets. With a holistic in-depth understanding of the organisation's capabilities they can make rapid instinctive decisions knowing they will be validated later by any rational financial analysis

We are not talking about gambling. In the same sense that the top athlete, golfer, tennis pro, quarter back, pitcher or other similar sports person can be 'in flow' or 'in the zone', so can the corporation with a sureness of instinct which is in itself a sustainable competitive advantage.

# 25

# The Financial Risk Factor & Treasury

No consideration of the management of risk would be complete without considering financial risk. Treasury has grown rapidly as a core profession in the corporation, particularly in the last 20 years. In many organisations, the treasury role once managed as part of the finance function now often sits as a role in its own right. Treasury directors are growing in number, especially in the financial service organisations and those corporations with substantial balance sheets such as the oil companies.

Having been a treasurer of a major financial services organisation, developing it from scratch as a key function, the proposal is that treasury should be the servant and facilitator, not master, in the management of risk process. As with mainstream finance it is important that all directors and senior managers understand the process and purpose of treasury. Certainly, treasury has responsibility to lead the financial engineering process and manage the cash and longer term financial assets. Increasingly, the function has become one of a portfolio investment function as part of the optimisation of balance sheet performance.

Although there may seem to be a somewhat tenuous connection, the Barings Bank example is one of the tail wagging the dog. Indeed there have been all too many examples in history where treasury overstepped the mark of balance sheet protection or investment, into the dangerous waters of speculation. Whether it be Rowntrees playing the cocoa market or a major Japanese chemical company becoming dangerously absorbed in derivatives, it ceases to be treasury when it loses sight of the central corporate objectives. Just as important as creating long-term value is sustaining such value.

### Balance Sheet Management

In our view, the prime objective of balance sheet management or asset/liability management should be:

*To optimise the total return on the balance
sheet at a managed level of risk.*

The prime focus should be on the protection of assets and viability. If any speculative activity is to take place, it should be a clearly defined process with a policy and objectives agreed at Board level. Accountability should also be actively pursued from Board level downwards. Added to this there should be clear separation of function and a tightly defined set of controls. Ideally an ALCO (Asset Liability Committee) should exist as a committee of the Board, reviewing not only the value creation processes but also the whole of the treasury function and purpose.

Once again, as the Barings Bank and other cases have shown, the Risk Factor in treasury is often the people - whether it be the directors ultimately held accountable or the manager who decided and implemented the day-to-day decisions. In Nick Leeson's case, he appears to have decided the plays, implemented them and managed the recording and funding of them with insufficient input at Board level.

## *The Financial Risk Factor*

The most obvious financial Risk Factor in treasury is volatility. Volatility continues to grow and can rapidly turn a profitable investment into significant loss before there is time to liquidate the position. By definition also, the use of derivatives is either to protect against or take advantage of volatility.

In the previous book, NLP for Investors and Traders, mention was made of one of the traditional investment protection strategies - the use of the stop-loss limits. In today's markets it is not uncommon for a profit warning to come out of the blue, sometimes leading to a fall of 25 per cent or more in the stock value. This level of volatility makes stop-loss limits sometimes difficult to sustain.

For the treasurer, just as much as the investor, the use of: a clearly defined strategy and policy; sophisticated techniques such as technical and fundamental analysis; a portfolio approach and; where appropriate, the use of derivatives to protect or enhance value; are among the tools and techniques available to minimise the financial Risk Factor.

The same sort of approaches we have advocated earlier in the use of the Risk Factor methodology to achieve sustained corporate and organisational success are relevant in treasury:

> We need a risk strategy to guide us as to the overall long-term purpose and perspective;

> We need a risk plan to manage the implementation of the agreed strategy within the determined policy;

> Risk information flow on what is happening to markets, investments, instruments, prices, the level of risk, the duration weighted value of the balance sheet, and the financial returns, etc. are fundamental;

> Risk education and training is equally fundamental. In the old days, many people ended up managing treasury by default, e.g. finance directors. Some of those were self-taught. With treasury having been professionalised for some time, and mistakes being so costly, training is inescapable;

> We need a risk process and structure in treasury to ensure e.g. separation of function and that too much power is not vested in one pair of hands;

> Risk recording, or the bookkeeping and regular monitoring of the portfolio are also basic requirements;

➤ Risk handling is shared between the treasurer and/or dealers and the brokers or principals being engaged in the market. There are many different risks that characterise the transaction processes, such as settlement risk;

➤ Risk assurance, or audit and compliance, are the means by which management and the Board can be certain that all of the above mechanisms are in place and working effectively.

Financial risk can be sub-divided into a number of different types of risk:

➤ Balance sheet risk is effectively a net exposure of the balance sheet to changing circumstances;

➤ Interest rate risk is in its simplest form the change in value of an asset or liability as a result of a change in interest rates;

➤ Credit risk is a reflection of the degree of exposure on a specific transaction or investment or the overall balance sheet to third party default or failure;

➤ Capital adequacy is a measure of the net amount of capital sufficient to cover the actual area or value of the risk of loss on the total balance sheet;

➤ Currency risk is the degree of exposure of a particular instrument or transactions or the balance sheet as a whole to changes in the values of currencies in which the assets and liabilities are reflected;

➤ Mismatches are where the nature, value, duration, interest rate basis (e.g. fixed or variable), etc. are different as between an asset and the liability which is deemed to fund it.

There are many other types of financial risk that it is the function of treasury to manage on a daily basis. Ignorance and abdication are no excuse where there is a significant net exposure or unexpected losses have occurred. It would be an astonishing piece of chance if any balance sheet was to be perfectly financially matched. Directors and managers often claim that it is not the policy to use financial engineering and derivatives. "We don't speculate" is the claim.

By doing nothing, you are by definition speculating because you are leaving your balance sheet exposed to the volatile forces of interest rates, currency rates, inflation, and other pricing factors, which will impact differentially between assets and liabilities.

Then there is cash flow management. It is no longer sufficient simply to plan for cash inflows and outflows to occur at the desired times. Not only are interest rates and currency rates varying all the time, but also for example, the shape of the interest rate yield curve (that is the level of interest rates for different periods of time) is not linear throughout the curve and is changing itself all the time. By discrete and carefully judged use of borrowing and investing it is possible to significantly increase the overall return on the balance sheet while still ensuring that cash funds are available when needed.

It is yet another example of the Risk Factor approach as opposed to prudence, caution or even neglect. Not understanding the treasury factors at work may either be increasing their speculative element or at the very least failing to optimise the balance sheet. Dabbling in treasury takes this a worrying step further. Adopting an insurance type approach, by minimising the risk, may well sustain the value in the balance sheet but does nothing for increasing long-term value even when security can also be preserved.

So treasury is a microcosm of the Risk Factor. Screw the balance sheet down for safety and achieve an average return. Understand and professionally manage all factors at work and achieve above average performance with no increased overall risk. Most of all, with treasury as with the whole organisation the Risk Factor approach leads to a better holistic understanding of the business with net benefits all round.

## *Insuring the Treasury Function*

Looked at from an insurance perspective there is a wide range of mechanisms available to protect from risk. Derivatives, while regarded by some as being highly risky instruments can be used with total safety to protect the value of an individual asset or liability, an expected cash flow or the balance sheet as a whole. Liquidity itself could be looked on as a type of insurance in that it is making sure that cash is always available for unexpected needs. Whilst being cautious by nature, liquidity can increase certainty of funding and avoid the opportunity cost of having to realise another investment for an unplanned eventuality.

For those businesses that make a regular practise of lending money to individuals or corporations, credit scoring is a means of insurance in the sense that it evaluates the risk before it is undertaken.

Fidelity insurance and key person insurance both in and outside the treasury function are ways of protecting against losses, which may arise where individuals make errors or commit fraud. No amount of such insurance would have been enough to protect against the sort of losses that Nick Leeson ran up. However, these would have been minimised through separation of function and tight control processes that are also by nature a form of insurance.

Whilst directors are ultimately individually and collectively accountable, the processes of overseeing the strategy and policy implementation and effectiveness of the controls are usually delegated to ALCO and the Audit Committee, respectively.

# 26

# The Risk Factor in Corporate 'Well-Being' - Safety, Security & Fraud

Let us take the analogy one stage further. What are the challenges or threats to our own well-being? Spiritual - motivation, self-esteem, morale, stability, relationships and external perception by others. Practical and physical - wealth and financial security, health, well-being, physical soundness, strength and security.

We have considered many of the spiritual Risk Factors in the corporate organisation. We have seen the importance of motivation, self-esteem and high morale as central to a successful culture. Once again these are focussed around the people factor. A self-esteeming, motivated organisation with high morale will not only be relatively stable but potentially capable of achieving differentiated success. In some respects, there are advantages in a positive instability. It would be fundamental to the ability of the corporation to continually reinvent itself.

As in our own lives, there are many relationships that are important to organisational success. 'Family' seems to have become less important outside the organisation as industries and sectors have become more disaggregated. Even trade associations and professional bodies have been losing some of their power and influence as different priorities have emerged for today's executives and managers. There is no cosy existence any more.

However, within the organisation 'family' is assuming much greater significance in two main respects. Leading edge management thinking is now reviewing the best models of family in society with a view to transporting those into the organisation. Outside the organisation, as the challenges for individual employees and managers escalate, such as longer working hours, more stress, variable job satisfaction, etc. the value of stability in personal relationships assumes increasing importance for the individual in an organisation.

The structure of the organisation itself has been breaking down, not in a negative sense but in a move towards semi-autonomous units, mother ship and satellite structures and the rapid growth in outsourcing, home working and self-employment. Furthermore, the astonishing growth in the use of call centres for both sales and service is part of a fundamental and irreversible change in the way the corporate body operates.

Before leaving the spiritual part of this analogy, let us consider the down sides of morale and self-esteem, and external perception by others.

As in life, there is a momentum in relationships. A successful, self-esteeming organisation can achieve extraordinary performance, especially where it is focussed around the continuing cycle of improvement and the ability to constructively examine and renew itself. Most people want to be associated with success. Successful, entrepreneurial organisations attract successful, entrepreneurial individuals. Taking Microsoft as an example, they can be highly motivated and highly rewarded.

Especially in what Tom Peters called "the nanosecond 90's" in a marketplace where Internet companies can grow to billions of pounds of stock market worth in no time at all, success, momentum and morale go hand in hand. When the bubble bursts, the momentum slows or fails, a company's high achievers may decide to move on to the next miracle.

Where so much is demanded of the individual, even more ordinary organisations can see their morale change overnight, finding they face a growing staff turnover rate and/or a haemorrhage of their best people. We have seen situations where even career enhancing positive challenges have not been sufficient to hold good people. Situations where they start to lose belief in management's ability to deliver, in their own value to the organisation or the potential total tangible and intangible reward package in relation to the effort expended.

External perceptions can also be critically important and here again we're talking about brand. You cannot put a price on the value to an individual member in an organisation that is being undeniably and visibly successful in the public eye. People like to be associated with success and on the contrary may not stay around to be associated with failure. Whilst there are some managers and executives who see a turnaround situation as one of life's greatest challenges, those who are in less of a position to influence corporate fortunes may not stick around when the going gets tough. Failing organisations are often characterised and staffed by mediocrity.

Once again, we are making the point that the people factor is fundamental whether from a positive or negative point of view. Text books abound with examples of best practise 'management by walking around', walking the talk, etc. Over and over again we have found that successful organisations are characterised by awareness and understanding of everything that is going on, challenge, interest and involvement, empowerment, initiative and enterprise. Such organisations are using the power of the people factor to their advantage. Risk, when fully understood can be turned to advantage.

## Physical Threats to the Corporate Body

The Risk Factors here are taken to include those, which represent a threat to the processes and systems of the organisation as well as its physical stability and security. In the latter respect, the issues to be aware of include the physical building, operations and personal security. Health and safety issues are now widely promulgated and regulated. Power supply and other utility resources are also critical.

Once again, to take the human analogy, what are the threats that we face daily as individuals? Physical security, hunger and lack of energy, illness, etc.

It still continues to surprise us that companies are daily wiped out by computer viruses and other associated technology failures. The software to protect against viruses and the maintenance and renewal regimes or technology have become relatively so cheap that it seems laziness and negligence must be key contributors. Once again, the people factor.

As far as physical security is concerned, it is people who overlook physical risk and also people who take advantage of an organisation's physical vulnerability.

Even the virtual organisation relies on people. Ironically, such companies that have successfully managed to reduce their dependence on a central resource may have thereby increased physical risk by dependence on a smaller group of key people. For large organisations, the now apparent annual flu epidemics have shown themselves capable of decimating corporate performance.

Any organisation working in the industry of, or capable of, creating a major health risk or public health risk has to take particular care. Look, for example, at BNFL (British Nuclear Fuels Ltd). Once again, the people factor was key. The widely publicised failure by a relatively junior group of people whose responsibility it was to carry out routine safety checks on a highly volatile product lead to a series of damaging consequences.

First of all, several major contracts were either put in peril or cancelled. As the seriousness of the situation became widely debated in the public domain, first the company's future as a separate entity became questioned and eventually top management was brought into the spotlight and some members were forced to go. This was the people factor in evidence in two respects: first their internal failings; and second the power of people's opinion in forcing change in an organisation which at first appeared not to understand the seriousness of its shortcomings.

With apparent global communications, more and more we see this pattern occurring. While we might spend a few moments debating the power of the media, at the end of the day people read and watch what they want to. We all have choices.

In terms of personal choices, other very real elements of the people factor in organisations include the daily regime of individual members of staff. Without a culture that encourages mental and physical fitness and occupational health, problems such as diet, drugs and alcohol, fitness for work and even accidents can escalate to the point where they are a threat to the company's well being.

Finally, the people factor also manifests itself in the processes for engaging, motivating, understanding and rewarding employees. Fraud, theft, malice and even viruses can be the product of failure in either the recruitment, engaging and understanding processes with people. It is not uncommon for people leaving organisations in negative circumstances to seek vengeance against their former employer. Whether this is by exposure in the media, or some malicious act, one individual can have a significant impact on both the viability and the brand.

# 27

# The Environmental Risk Factor

The environmental Risk Factor is an unavoidable consideration, as a result of stakeholder attitudes, including public opinion, especially with regard to irreplaceable natural resources, public health and safety. Ignorance is no excuse.

There is no need to document here the different types of environmental risk. If any organisation is unaware of these, it is missing one of the most significant changes at the start of the 21st century. It is not just a matter of physical damage to the environment or the organisation itself, it is also closely associated with brand and reputation. Again, we cite the Union Carbide example.

For many companies it becomes a case of balancing the holistic costs of compliance with legislation and best practise against the practical and intangible consequences of breaking the law. To take another example, even though Shell had done a thorough review of all the options available to them with regard to the disposal of an obsolete North Sea oil rig, and was later shown to have chosen a sound environmental option, Greenpeace and public opinion managed to persuade it to change his mind.

While the practical and financial consequences of prosecution for environmental pollution, for example, do not yet pose a serious enough threat to persuade some organisations to change their practices, it is the growing power of media and public opinion, which represents the longer-term challenge. Again, brand and reputation may be paramount.

Even though global environmental challenges abound and grow daily, the ability of an individual or many organisations to have a material impact is still limited. What is needed is a collective will to produce fundamental change. In the meantime, legislation, especially in Europe, where e.g. the Green party had extraordinary success in Germany, may begin to change attitudes and practices.

While the Risk Factor for public reputation and brand may have the greatest long-term consequences, it is both difficult to predict and quantify. It may prove increasingly difficult to divert or deflect some of these risks with a growing difficulty of insurance. Green competitiveness factors have been having an effect for some years now. Although the craze for environmental investment media has abated for the time being, people are becoming increasingly interested in the policies adopted by organisations that they transact with or invest in.

A good example in the UK is the Co-op bank. Despite being a financial services organisation, with no manufacturing or distribution interest whatsoever, the Co-op bank has determined and applied environmentally friendly and community involvement policies in its relationships with all of its stakeholders. Although it remains as something of an anomaly in being a mutual bank, it has managed to create for itself a niche in the marketplace, resulting in differentiated performance.

There is no doubt that the public is becoming more aware of and more concerned about pollution, contamination, accidents, toxic and hazardous products. What is most interesting is the growth of a NIMBY (Not In My BackYard) attitude to many of the 'dirty' aspects of business, extending as far as industrial or commercial development in the green belt.

Energy friendly policies as well as being legislated are becoming widespread practice in both individuals' homes and businesses. With green taxation policies growing especially in Europe, energy costs have become both an efficiency and an environment consideration. For the time being, public initiatives may be having more effect on control and disposal of waste than legislation. But as time goes on, organisations will become even more interested in suppliers' environmental policies.

Eco labelling, environmentally friendly packaging and stationery are other aspects of the practical implementation of the environmental Risk Factor. The shorter-term costs may be a worthwhile investment, especially as so much of brand is subliminal. New products are emerging daily which explicitly or implicitly take account of environmental factors. Pressure groups are no longer operating at the fringes of society and many have now moved into the mainstream of public opinion.

Consciously or unconsciously, global warming and climate change are a serious long-term threat to society, industry and the individual. We are already seeing some of the effects in the unpredictability of climate: by increasing violence and volatility of the weather; the breakdown of traditional seasonal patterns; the growing difficulty of predicting the need for and pattern of the energy requirements. In the meantime, whilst oil has retained its pre-eminence for the time being due to continuing dependence on the internal combustion engine, we may need to begin to redefine the term scarce resources.

Burning oil in its various forms is a major environmental threat. Whether through supply and demand factors or the growing practice of punitive taxes it may become a scarce resource. In the meantime, public pressure groups are having a growing impact on the nuclear power industry throughout the world. With alternative energy sources for the time being having a far higher unit cost, all these and other elements of the environmental Risk Factor will increasingly impinge on the practices and viability of the corporation. One of the most obvious aspects will be the change in transport policies, infrastructure, usage, mix and patterns of movement.

➣        ➣        ➣

# 28

# Disasters & Contingencies

No discussion of risk would be complete without a consideration of disasters and contingencies. Our assumption here would be that a disaster is beyond the control of the organisation. In other words we are implicitly saying that a broad and detailed understanding of the significance of managing all the Risk Factors in the business excludes the possibility of disaster as a consequence of failed control or negligence.

Key questions therefore are:

➤ What insurance arrangements, and diversion or deflection of risk have already taken place?

➤ What Risk Factor planning, preparation and management arrangements exist to minimise the possibility or consequences of potential disasters?

Contingency planning should be an integral part of the planning and operational processes. Any understanding of the holistic aspects of the business, together with all of the other Risk Factors leads to the probability that the organisation will have considered most possible contingencies and how it will plan or react in a controlled manner if they occur.

The first fundamental is continuation of business. It appears that some organisations believe it is sufficient to acquire consequential loss insurance. The question is do you want to recover the value of the business or do you want to continue in business as you were?

Assuming the latter is the answer, then an understanding and consideration of the Risk Factors may be the way to avoid most possible contingencies ever occurring.

You can insure against fire, water, electrical, contamination and other loss or damage. The question is, what are the wider consequences for the business and its continuity, especially those not necessarily directly affected by the incident. For example, electrical failure or water damage could lead to a temporary or permanent loss of computer systems processing.

In this day and age it is more often the inability to continue to process data, which ultimately brings an organisation down. Even where software packages have been bought off the shelf, they are inevitably integrated into the daily operational systems and processes. In addition to this there is the risk of permanent loss of data and records.

## The People Factor

We make no apology for returning again to the people factor. With both litigation and damages increasing on both sides of the Atlantic for personal injury or death, the insured consequences for individuals in the organisation or the public at large could cause lasting or even terminal damage to corporate viability.

Many years ago, during an extraordinary weather event in Bradford, a flash flood that followed caused many of the cellars in the city to fill with water. In the city centre, subways were flooded to the roof. Nearby, at the headquarters of the Provincial building society, hundreds of thousands of mortgage deeds were put at risk because they were stored in the basement. An emergency team was sent down to recover them. As the people stood waist deep in water, management suddenly realised that the electricity supply was still connected. Fortunately, nobody suffered any injury but this is a real practical example of the need for the wider consideration of the Risk Factors.

Kidnap, ransom and extortion have become an occasional factor in public life. Very often, a person threatened is either a key manager or owner of a business, or a member of the family. Although the size of the demand could put the business at risk, there is no doubt where the priority should be.

Allied Colloids had a major chemical factory based in a residential district of West Yorkshire. A fire and consequent chemical leakage threatened nearby homes with damage and inhalation problems. Many homes had to be evacuated. The company not only suffered financial loss and loss of business continuity, but also ended up being prosecuted, with consequent effect on its brand and reputation and the position of the Chief Executive.

Over and over again, the Risk Factors and their consequences extend far beyond the apparent immediate perception. Invariably, the people factor is the most significant of all, whether directly or as a consequence.

It would be no exaggeration to say that every single organisation should have the equivalent of a disaster and contingency plan. In even the smallest of businesses, very often the biggest single risk to its stability and viability is the dependence on the owner or General Manager.

*All of the appendices in **The Risk Factor**, plus a number of other useful templates can be downloaded in larger format from www.TheRiskFactor.com*

# Appendix 1
# Questionnaire - How Are We Doing?

The Risk Factor Questionnaire - How are we are doing?

| Key Risk Factors | A | B | C | D | E | F | G | H |
|---|---|---|---|---|---|---|---|---|
| Core Elements | | | | | | | | |
| 1  Strategy | | | | | | | | |
| 2  (Action) Planning | | | | | | | | |
| 3  Information Flow | | | | | | | | |
| 4  Education (& Training) | | | | | | | | |
| 5  (Process) Structure | | | | | | | | |
| 6  Recording | | | | | | | | |
| 7  Handling | | | | | | | | |
| 8  Assurance (Audit & Compliance | | | | | | | | |
| The Key Risk Factors | A  Financial Implications | B  Decision Making | C  Process & Structure | D  People (& Machines) | E  Legal & Regulatory | F  Customer / Clients | G  Environmental | H  Communication |

Please photocopy this chart and transfer it to an OHP transparency to enable one chart to be overlaid to another similar chart but with a different combination of (fascias)

# Appendix 2
# The Context of Risk
# - A Strategic Planning Template

An outline Strategic Planning process, incorporating risk considerations, as a basis for dynamic strategic planning and evaluation.

## Mission and Vision

- What is the corporate mission and vision?
- What has happened since the last review, which might threaten or undermine these and lead to fundamental review, revision or abandonment?
- What strategic decisions would we have to make if there has been fundamental change?
- What is the proposed revised vision/mission?
- What is the likelihood of acceptance by our investors, customers, stakeholders and employees?

## Definition of Business

- What business and core market(s) are we in?
- What new strategic factors threaten that business or those markets, or should we take account of?
- What challenges do these pose?
- What are the likely business and financial consequences?
- What should we consider changing?
- What would lead us to question or abandon our mission, vision and purpose?

## What is our Business Philosophy and Ethos? What is our Corporate Culture?

- What are our attitudes to our customers, investors, stakeholders, business, core markets, business, political, economic and social environment?
- What changes have taken place in these?
- How, if at all, would this change our attitudes?

- What are our core beliefs?
- How have the above 'environmental' changes, or any challenges to our mission, vision, purpose, business, or core markets affected our core beliefs, if at all?
- What business and personal values, agreed among ourselves and with our major stakeholders, do we hold up to challenge?
- What challenges or threats do they face?
- What changes or redefinition would we consider?
- How do our attitudes, beliefs and values affect our collective, corporate behaviour?
- What business philosophy and ethos do we construct from the above?
- What fundamental challenges do these face, if any?

## Corporate Distinctiveness and Brand

- What are the critical elements of our Brand?
- What is our corporate image? How do our stakeholders regard us?
- What distinctive competences do we have, locally or globally, in our chosen business and markets?
- What challenges do these face? What new entrants are there to challenge us? What are their distinctive competences?
- What competitive advantages do we hold in our chosen business and strategic markets?
- What new threats are there to these and our distinctive competences?
- What action do we propose in response to the above?
- Do any of these challenges require us to rethink our mission, vision, purpose, core business, culture and philosophy, key strategic markets, product strategy or any other critical aspect of our business and strategy?

## Goals and Corporate Objectives

- What is our 3/5 year goal?
- What is our 1 year goal?
- What changes or challenges in any of the above strategic considerations would cause us to rethink or re-evaluate these goals?
- What are our key corporate objectives?
- For whom do we hold these objectives?

- Who are our key stakeholders: investors and shareholders; customers; employees; suppliers; government and regulatory relationships; public agencies; etc?

## What is our chosen overall Corporate Direction and Strategy?

- What do the forecasts and trends for our markets tell us about the prospects for the next 1/3 years?
- What do they tell us about cost and other economic factors relevant to our business targets?
- What significant changes have there been in any of these since we last examined them?
- How, if at all, would these change our goals, our key strategies or our immediate tactics?
- What are the significant strengths and weaknesses of our organisation and its business?
- Who are the existing, new or potential competitors that we should be aware or concerned about?
- What are those equivalent factors for our significant competitors?
- What, if any, changes can we discern in the factors for our competitors, either now, or projected?
- What are the opportunities and threats in our political, economic, social and technological environment?
- What significant changes have there been since we last reviewed these?
- What significant changes have there been in the markets in which we operate?
- What new markets have emerged which we should consider (i.e. as being tangential to our existing markets, or markets into which we might move to add lasting long-term value, without fundamentally changing our core mission, vision and goals)?
- What significant current or forecast changes in consumer behaviour have occurred, which may affect how we operate in our main markets, or may produce new opportunities in the future, in keeping with our core mission, vision and goals?
- What new product opportunities have emerged, or can be created, as a result of any of the above?
- Are there any products or markets from which we should withdraw, as being uneconomic, in light of the forecasts and projections arising out of the foregoing review of our environment, business, markets and products?

- What changes to our existing strategy, if any, should we consider as a result of the foregoing review?
- What different scenarios should we consider in deciding whether to vary our corporate direction and strategy?
- What alternative strategies present themselves for consideration?
- What are the business and financial consequences of the evaluation of these alternative strategies?
- What are the key strategic issues that arise from this review of our overall corporate direction and strategy?
- What fundamental strategic decisions do we need to consider as a result?
- In summary, what are the key strategic opportunities, challenges, risks and consequences that face us now and in the next 3 years?
- What will be our response to these?
- In summary, how would these considerations affect the financial projections for the organisation's performance?
- What financial challenges and risks arise as a result of this quantification?
- How will we meet these challenges: iterate all the foregoing in the context of the financial constraints and revise our strategy; manage the identified financial challenges and risks within the projected financial constraints, without prejudice to the viability of the business; insure against certain risks in order to reduce the financial risk profile?

**In summary, what is the portfolio of corporate strategic decisions, their attendant revenue, cost, cashflow, profit, business and financial risk profiles?**

- When we review this portfolio of decisions, how, if at all, can we vary the overall strategic mix, in order to optimise the reward/risk profile?
- What, if any, other considerations arise out of the foregoing, especially potential effects on our brand, corporate image or public profile, with our key stakeholders, or our business direction, ethos and philosophy, corporate values or long-term competitive advantage?
- What, if any, modifications would we make to the above confirmed or revised strategic direction, as a result of these 'macro' strategic consequences?

## Business Development and Investment

*Business as Usual*

● What, if any, are the additional challenges, opportunities and risks we need to take account of in our 'business as usual' i.e. the part of our planned business that represents 'more of the same'?

● What, if any, are the business or financial consequences which arise as a result?

● What is the amount of capital available for investment in the business?

● What is the planned disposition of that capital at present?

● What capital changes are necessary as a result of the projected or planned changes in our business as usual?

● How much capital does this leave (if any) for business development or business investment?

*Business Development*

● What changes could we make to our existing business that would increase the efficiency or reduce the risk profile without reducing the projected net returns or adversely affecting cash flow?

● How could we improve the quality of our management and business processes without incremental risk or adverse financial consequences?

● How could we redesign or add new processes, to improve the quality and/or profitability of the business, without potential adverse risk and financial consequences?

● What capital changes arise out of the above, while still leaving positive incremental profit and cash flow, without incremental risk or future adverse financial consequences?

● How much capital does this leave for business investment?

*Business Investment*

● What new markets or new products are open to us as a result of our strategic considerations?

● What capital investment would be needed in order to facilitate these business investments?

● What could or should we cease doing (business disinvestments), the net result of which would improve our overall profitability and cash flow, without future adverse risk or financial consequences?

- What strategic or business alliances should we consider, in keeping with the review of our overall strategic direction, which would add overall long-term value, without adverse strategic, financial or risk consequences in the future?
- What is our core business?
- What aspects of our business processes do we no longer need to do at all, or can safely and effectively contract out to other producers, manufacturers or service suppliers, in order to increase profitability and long-term value, without adverse effects on cash flow, financial or risk consequences in the future?
- What mergers, acquisitions or other strategic investments should we consider, in order to secure or improve our long-term value adding capability, without adversely affecting future cash flows, financial or risk consequences?
- What are the capital consequences of the above?
- What are the overall capital consequences of all of the above business developments and investments?
- What are the overall financial, funding and risk consequences of all the above proposals?
- How, if at all, would this proposed programme of capital changes affect our overall ability to deliver our mission, vision and corporate goals through our chosen strategic direction?
- What would we need to reconsider in either the overall strategic direction, the proposed capital programme, or the funding, financial and risk management consequences of either?

## Practical Consequences of the Chosen Strategic Direction

- What Resources do we need in order to implement this chosen direction, in terms of:
  - Capital;
  - Organisation and infrastructure;
  - People - strategic and operational managers and implementers;
  - Physical assets;
  - Cash flow requirements.
- What changes do we need in the above, as a result of the new challenges, opportunities, new or revised strategic direction and their consequences.
- How are we going to implement the chosen or revised strategic direction?

> Through what new or revised management and business processes;

> Through what information and telecommunication systems to support the management and business processes;

● What are the incremental Risk Factors associated with the above changes? What are the possible effects on long-term added value?

● What are the Critical Success Factors that will determine or inhibit the success in delivering our chosen strategic direction?

● What are the short medium and long-term targets for performance?

● By what measures - Key Performance Indicators and Benchmarks of performance, integrated into a balanced scorecard of qualitative and quantitative measures - will we know we are successful in delivering our strategy, or that we need to review or change direction?

**Communication of Strategic Direction, Progress and Key Decisions**

● Through what media and by what means shall we ensure that everyone understands what we are trying to do and how we are doing?

● Through what processes shall we ensure that we receive feedback on the business and progress against our goals and targets for performance?

● How shall we audit the effectiveness of these communication processes?

● How shall we ensure that we receive all the feedback we need, from which we can help determine where we can improve the delivery of our agreed strategic direction?

**Continuous Improvement**

● What are the challenges and risks to the achievement of the above?

● What are the opportunities to augment or otherwise improve our ability to deliver our mission through achievement of our medium and long-term goals, by modifying, replacing or augmenting our chosen strategic direction?

# Appendix 3

# The Total Cost of Risk - A Working Template

As with the Strategic Planning Template, the following is based on questions. It is not intended that these should be prescriptive, although they could in fact be used as the basis for risk review in any management process. The important thing is that management has the right focus and the organisation has an intuitive risk-aware culture, in which to implement the actions that lead to incremental long-term value.

**People**

- What is the most appropriate organisation structure in order to implement the plan?
- What is the most efficient set of discrete management processes to implement the plan?
- What competences do we need in order to implement or support this part of the strategic plan?
- What is the most efficient way to group these competences in discrete roles, in order to implement the relevant processes?
- What competences set do we already have, within the management group of the organisation?
- What gaps are there in these competences, without which we shall be unable to implement or flex the plan as agreed?
- How are we going to recruit or develop those competences?
- What excess competences do we have after matching the plan implementation?
- How are we going to retrain, redispose, 'warehouse' or release those competences? Are any of them likely to be needed for the future?
- What is the holding, retraining or redisposal cost of these human resources?
- What is the choice, which optimises long-term value?
- What are the risks within the plan period, that there will be insufficient human resources, especially in terms of specific skills and competences, to deliver the strategic plan?
- What are the risks and possible consequences of key personnel during the period?

- What contingency plans are in process, to protect against these possible risks, including training and development of alternative or complementary skills?
- What steps are taken to ensure that roles are neither over- nor under- specified, leading to excess cost or insufficient skills and competences?
- Which processes are highly or over-dependent on one, a few, or key personnel in order to continue to be performed effectively?
- Which processes are interdependent on these high-risk processes?
- How flexible are reward and remuneration policies, in order to take account of the possible effects of competition, scarcity of resources or the need to incentivise and retain key personnel?
- How dependent are operational processes on staff or key personnel understanding complex, highly skilled or technical processes, procedures or systems?
- How effective are HR policies and procedures in providing for recruitment needs, or identifying performance in order to provide appropriate rewards and incentives?
- Is there a Manpower, Training and Development plan?
- How well have managers identified and understood the HR risks in their own processes?
- What HR resources exist to anticipate, respond to and manage risks when they arise, including where necessary contracting or managing the use of external expertise or resources?

## Processes

- What is the definition of this process?
- What is the purpose of this process?
- How does it contribute to the delivery of the agreed strategic direction and long-term value?
- What other processes does it interact with?
- What other processes depend on this process for value added inputs?
- What other processes does this process depend on in order to produce value added outputs?
- What are the risks inherent in this process?
- What other processes would be impacted by these risks occurring?

- What is the value added from this process over the plan period?
- What is the potential value of the possible risks?
- What is the probability of each risk occurring, over what time frames?
- What are the alternatives to managing each risk?
- What are the costs of each alternative?
- What is the optimum way forward, in terms of long-term added value?
- What is the recommended decision and the basis for its selection?
- What other possible risks were identified as a result of this risk evaluation?
- Which process(as) should be informed of these possible risks?
- Which of these decisions, considerations or possible consequences, including financial, should be reported to senior management or those responsible for managing financial risks and processes?
- What, if any concerns arise which should be immediately considered by the Board or Audit Committee (if the latter exists)?

## Systems

*Development Risks*

- Is there an IT Strategic Plan to co-ordinate and match the systems needs of the organisation?
- What process exists to understand, anticipate and plan for possible changes in information technology, including obsolescence or improvement of delivery systems?
- What process exists to understand, consider, recommend and plan for the implementation of new systems where appropriate?
- Is there a corporate set of IT/IS standards, including a corporate buying policy and the means to ensure the effective integration of any new IT, IS or telecommunications?
- What process exists to understand management and business processes across the organisation and anticipate the need for new or modified supporting systems?

*Errors*

- What risks are there in data entry, development and amendment of programmes, systems design, and routine systems procedures, the customisation and use of software packages, etc.

- What process exists to ensure these are understood, anticipated and managed in accordance with the delivery of the strategic plan, at an optimum incremental cost to long-term value?
- What processes and supporting systems exist to ensure that all system implementation or modification is agreed and tested before implementation?

*Business Interruption*

- What systems and processes exist to identify errors as, or even before they occur?
- What is this information system?
- Which process(es) does it support?
- What are the risks inherent in the system?
- What are the other possible risks to this system?
- What is the probability of each risk occurring?
- What is the potential loss of value, or cost of each risk?
- What are the possible courses of action to secure this system?
- What are the projected costs for each course of action?
- What is the optimum way forward for each potential risk?
- What is the recommended decision and the basis for its selection?
- Which process will take this decision and how will it inform affected parties and/or commission the necessary action?
- What other possible risks have been identified as a result of this risk analysis?
- Which process(es) should be informed of these possible risks?
- What concerns, if any, should be reported direct to the Board or Audit Committee?

## Finance

- Which financial process is being reviewed?
- Which management process(es) does it support?
- What are the financial consequences, in terms of cash flow, return and cost, of this financial process?
- What are the financial risks implicit in these transactions?
- What are the financial consequences of these risks?
- What is the probability of each of these risks?
- What are the possible courses of action to manage, hedge, or neutralise these risks?
- What are the financial consequences, in terms of cash flow, return and cost for each of these possible courses of action?

- What is the optimum course of action in each case, in terms of long-term added value?
- What is the recommended course of action in each case and the basis for the decision?
- Which other financial processes are affected by this process and/or course of action?
- What are the possible complementary or additional financial consequences for these related financial processes, arising out of this recommended course of action?
- Have these other financial processes considered these possible consequences and decided on possible courses of action?
- What is the net overall effect on cash flow, return and costs, in terms of long-term added value, when all the related financial courses of action are taken into account?
- Would this overall summary, modify or negate any of the proposed courses of action?
- What, if any of the above consideration, courses of action, or financial consequences need to be reported to senior management before being effected, i.e. as being potentially of strategic importance or material in value in relation to the overall financial prospects of the organisation?

**Insurance Template**

Before contemplating insuring any risk outside the organisation, the following questions should be asked:
- In which process might this risk occur?
- What is the nature of the possible risk?
- What is the probability of the risk occurring?
- What is the potential value of the occurrence, in terms of reduced revenue, increased or unforeseen costs?
- What is the potential effect on cash flow?
- What are the possible courses of action to manage this risk, in terms of:
  - Being constantly vigilant for the possible incidence of the risk and managing proactively as appropriate;
  - Removing the source of risk immediately?
  - Neutralising the risk, for example by hedging it?
  - Insuring against the eventuality;
  - Ignoring the risk completely (i.e. consciously self-insuring it).

- Where insurance is being contemplated, what are the possible courses available, whether through a broker, or directly with the underwriting market?
- What are the potential effects of each possible course of action, in terms of loss of revenue increased costs and cash flow?
- What is the optimum course of action in terms of its effect on long-term added value?
- What is the recommended decision, supported by the above analysis?

## Appendix 4
## Chart - Scoring the Chapter Questions

List all questions from each Chapter in the form of a questionnaire as outlined below.

| Chapter | 6 | 5 | 4 | 3 | 2 | 1 | 0 |
|---|---|---|---|---|---|---|---|
| Questions | Yes / No | Yes / No | Yes / No | Yes / No | Yes / No | Yes / No | Yes / No |
| List 1 a-h | | | | | | | |
| List 2 a-h | | | | | | | |
| List 3 a-h | | | | | | | |
| List 4 a-h | | | | | | | |
| List 5 a-h | | | | | | | |
| List 6 a-h | | | | | | | |
| List 7 a-h | | | | | | | |
| List 8 a-h | | | | | | | |
| **Totals** | | | | | | | |

## Appendix 5
## Defining The Terminology for Your Organisation

Meanings & Explanations
➤     Risk Control = ...................................................................
➤     Assessing Risk = ...........................................................
➤     Managing Risk = ..........................................................
➤     Management of risk = .....................................................
➤     What other terms or meanings are relevant, or important in your own organisation?

................................................................
................................................................
................................................................
................................................................
................................................................
................................................................
................................................................
................................................................

All of the appendices in *The Risk Factor*, plus a number of other useful templates can be downloaded in larger format from www.TheRiskFactor.com